WINNERS

WINNERS

WOMEN AND THE NOBEL PRIZE

by Barbara Shiels

Dillon Press, Inc.
Minneapolis, Minnesota 55415

For my parents
Charlotte and Robert Johnston
two achievers

Library of Congress Cataloging in Publication Data

Shiels, Barbara.
    Winners : women and the Nobel Prize.

    Includes bibliographies and index.
    Summary: Biographies of eight women who have won the
Nobel Prize, with an introduction to Alfred Nobel and the prize
and a complete listing of female winners.
    1. Nobel prizes—Juvenile literature.   2. Women in the
professions—Biography—Juvenile literature.   [1. Nobel
prizes. 2. Women in the professions]   I. Title.
AS911.N9S48   1985   001.4'4'0922 [B] [920] 84-23036
ISBN 0-87518-293-3

Dillon Press, Inc., 242 Portland Avenue South
Minneapolis, Minnesota 55415

Printed in the United States of America
1 2 3 4 5 6 7 8 9 10 94 93 92 91 90 89 88 87 86 85

Contents

Acknowledgments

This book was made possible in part through a grant from the American Association of University Women Educational Foundation.

Interviews and correspondence with living Nobel winners and with relatives and friends of both living and deceased winners provided valuable firsthand materials. I also appreciate the help of experts in the fields of physics, chemistry, medicine, literature, and peace who offered informative criticism for pertinent chapters. I would especially like to thank two Nobel winners: Rosalyn S. Yalow and Dorothy Crowfoot Hodgkin. In addition, I am most grateful to: Robert G. Sachs (Director, The Enrico Fermi Institute, The University of Chicago) and Dean L. Mitchell (Division of Materials Research, National Science Foundation) for assistance with the Maria Goeppert Mayer chapter; Eileen Egan (author) for assistance with the Mother Teresa chapter; Sissela Bok (daughter), Stellan Andersson (Arbetarrörelsens Arkiv, Stockholm, Sweden), and Allan C. Carlson (Executive Vice President, The Rockford Institute) for assistance with the Alva Myrdal chapter; Jenny P. Glusker (Fox Chase Cancer Center) and Carolyn Lavallee and Leon Hawkins (South Lakes High School, Reston, Virginia) for assistance with the Dorothy Crowfoot Hodgkin chapter; Vera Lachmann (associate) and

Evelyn Pugh (Professor of History, George Mason University) for assistance with the Nelly Sachs chapter; Nora Stirling (author) for assistance with the Pearl Buck chapter; and Harriet B. Creighton (Emeritus Professor of Botany, Wellesley College), Marjorie McKinley (sister), Marjorie Bhavnani (niece), William Provine (Professor of History and member of the Division of Biological Sciences, Section of Ecology and Systematics, Cornell University), Bruce Wallace (University Distinguished Professor in Genetics, Virginia Polytechnic Institute and State University), and Ruth Sager (Professor of Cellular Genetics, Harvard Medical School) for assistance with the Barbara McClintock chapter.

I would like to acknowledge invaluable help from the staff of the Library of Congress: in particular, Constance Carter, Head of the Reference Section, Science & Technology Division; Sarah Pritchard, Reference Specialist in Women's Studies; and Robert W. Schaaf, Senior Specialist in United Nations and International Documents.

Thanks also go to The Leo Baeck Institute; Somerville College, Oxford, England; Michelle Aldrich (Director, Project for Women in Science, American Association for the Advancement of Science); Larilyn Reitnauer, Swedish Embassy, Washington, D.C.; Sarah Lawrence College; the staff of Reston Regional Library, Reston, Virginia, and in particular, Elizabeth A. Butler and Veronica O'Donnell; Fairfax County School librarians, Fairfax County, Virginia, and in particular Shirley Lenti and Washington Independent Writers.

Appreciation is expressed to Vita Pariente and her late husband, Art; Walter Froehlich; Andrea Kerr; Candice Ransom; Anna-Berta Page; Yvonne Leifert; and Isabel Wells. To my husband, Lawrence, go special thanks for supporting my work in numerous ways, especially for helping with research. My daughter, Hilary, started me on this project with a question and encouraged me throughout.

Those I asked for assistance contributed more time and information than I requested. It was their graciousness and generosity that enabled me to write this book.

I would also like to acknowledge the assistance of the publishers, institutions, and individuals that granted permission to reproduce

Introduction

The women whose life stories are in this book could be called twentieth-century heroines. They are adventurers who make journeys of the mind in laboratories, at typewriters, on crowded city streets, and in classrooms. In their work they have shown courage and leadership, and their achievements have changed many aspects of our lives. Above all, they have confidence. It takes confidence to experiment with atoms, cells, human relations, or words.

These women winners have other things in common, too, although—because each has followed an independent course—there are a few exceptions.

When they were growing up, most of the women winners enjoyed an affectionate relationship with their mothers, but they remember their fathers as the most important people in their early years. Fathers and daughters talked together, exchanging viewpoints and ideas. They also shared hobbies or the companionship of special times together. While, for the most part, the fathers were not prominent in the fields the girls would later choose to enter, they encouraged their daughters to get good educations, use their minds, and think about pursuing careers.

When they were young many of the future winners spent a great deal of time reading. But they also entered into the same activities—including sports and going out on dates—as other girls their age.

Quite early in life, usually during their teenage years, they realized they had a very strong interest in one particular area. They found they received good marks in certain subjects in school, or they spent a lot of their free time doing something that fascinated them—whether that was experimenting with chemicals or writing poetry. As they found out more about their special fields, they became skilled in the areas that were closely related to their interests. A few years later, making a decision about what career to follow usually was easy. One winner, Rosalyn S. Yalow, remembering her first awareness of her interest in science, says, "I just wasn't good at anything else."

Once the future winners knew what they wanted to learn, they pursued their studies with determination. Most encountered some form of discrimination against women if they attempted to gain admission to college and then to graduate school. They managed to attend these institutions, however, if their chosen field required a higher education. World War II provided a career boost for many of the winners since it created educational and employment opportunities for women.

These determined young women managed to complete their studies and enter the job market. Usually their work started in a quiet way. Many were given a tiny office or a small portion of a laboratory when they found their first position.

11

After becoming established in their fields, most of the winners reached a turning point in their professional lives. For some it came earlier than for others. Each woman experienced this crucial period in a different way, but each later acknowledged its importance.

For example, Alva Myrdal (Peace Prize 1982) became active in international diplomacy after concentrating earlier on social reforms in Sweden. Rosalyn S. Yalow (Physiology or Medicine Prize 1977) extended her original work in physics by working jointly with an expert in medicine. Nelly Sachs (Literature Prize 1966) began writing poetry that would bring her recognition only after she was forced to flee the horrors of Nazi-ruled Germany. A nun who would soon be known as Mother Teresa (Peace Prize 1979) left a sheltered convent in India to help the poor and desperately ill people of Calcutta's streets. Maria Goeppert Mayer (Physics Prize 1963) began her award-winning work when she decided to study nuclear physics, a field new to her.

While these career turning points changed the lives of the winners, it was their unwavering dedication to their work that set them apart from others in their chosen fields. No matter what else happened to them, they found what they wanted to do, learned how to do it well, and continued to do it. The majority experienced the same life events as other women—they married, had children, and endured illnesses. And, because they were only human, they also made their share of mistakes. But—through the event-filled years—they pursued their work. It gave them a deep sense of accomplishment.

Winners of Nobel Prizes receive the world's most prestigious award. Overnight they become as popular as movie stars. No matter how much their coworkers have noticed them before, nothing equals the attention they now receive. Every aspect of their lives is examined in print and on the air; anything unfavorable is revealed to all eyes.

The winners react in various ways to their celebrity status. Some accept invitations to make speeches, appear on television, and receive more awards. Others retreat to their desks or laboratories as soon as the first wave of publicity ends.

Each year that another woman's name appears on the list of winners, reporters rush to her home. One of the first questions they ask her is: "What makes you so remarkable?" The Nobel winner always finds it difficult to answer. To her, her life seems perfectly ordinary. "I work, enjoy my family and friends, love and care for others," is the gist of her reply. "There's nothing different about what I do."

Yet, as the life stories of the women in this book show, Nobel winners—whether they realize it or not—represent a rare commitment to excellence. They have changed our world by improving health care, increasing the chance for peace, developing new technological tools, and interpreting the human experience. Achievement, they find, brings its own satisfaction. That is why many of the winners say the real thrill comes from the work that leads to a Nobel Prize rather than from the prize itself.

Alfred Nobel

and the Nobel Prizes

The remarkable story of Alfred Nobel and the Nobel Prizes began in Sweden in the 1830s and continues today. Nobel's life, his surprising will, and the establishment of the prizes set the stage for a drama that unfolds every year. What names will be next on the list of winners? The answer comes each fall when a fortunate few learn they have been selected. The prizes bring worldwide prestige and lasting glory to those honored.

Alfred Nobel: The Man Behind the Prizes

Inventions were a tradition in the Nobel family. When Alfred was born in Stockholm, Sweden, in 1833, his father Immanuel had a reputation for developing unusual devices. Once he designed a rubber backpack that could be used as an air mattress, a life jacket, and a section of a floating bridge. But Immanuel failed to find a market for this and other of his inventions.

In 1837 he went bankrupt, left his homeland, Sweden,

and traveled to Russia. His wife and sons—Alfred and two older boys—remained behind. This time Immanuel was successful. He established a machine shop and soon had a rapidly expanding business.

He sent for his wife and sons, and the family lived in Saint Petersburg (now called Leningrad). A year later another son, Emil, was born. In Russia Alfred was taught by private tutors and attended school for only one year. He never went to a university and, like his father, taught himself much of what he knew.

By the time he was a young man, his knowledge was extraordinary. An excellent scientist, he also knew and liked literature and was fluent in five languages. When he was seventeen, his father sent him abroad to complete his education. In Europe and the United States, he observed the work of engineers and industrialists.

Back in Russia, Alfred began work at his father's factory where production was booming. His two older brothers also were in the family business. The Nobels by now were leading suppliers of armaments and ammunition for Russian fighting forces preparing for the Crimean War. Alfred became fascinated by the explosives he worked with, and, when still young, obtained a patent for a discovery of his own. This was a process by which a powerful explosive, nitroglycerine, could be detonated, or suddenly exploded, in a controlled blast by a percussive cap. The discovery, Alfred was the first to point out, had many peaceful uses: blasting rock in quarries, constructing bridges, and building roads.

At the end of the Crimean War the family's fortunes were again reversed. Immanuel's business closed down. He, his wife, and Emil returned to Sweden. The three older sons were left to carry on in Russia. All three brothers eventually became famous. Robert became the head of a giant petroleum industry, and Ludwig founded an arms factory. Alfred remained fascinated by explosives.

By 1865 businesses all over Europe were interested in buying Alfred's blasting material. Things looked hopeful until disaster struck. One day an explosion ripped through a small factory Immanuel had set up when he returned to Sweden. Five people were killed, one of whom was Emil who had been working with the new explosive. A month later Immanuel suffered a stroke and never fully recovered.

Until then no one had thought there was great risk involved with Alfred's invention. Now, however, there was widespread fear. Orders were cancelled. Then a Swedish millionaire came to Alfred's assistance, and the family business was reestablished. Because the explosive worked, it sold well. Before long, Nobel factories sprang up all over Europe.

Alfred went to the United States and started a company there. When more accidents occurred, he became determined to change the explosive itself so that it would be safer to transport and use. After trying various substances, he found a sandy clay and mixed it with nitroglycerine. The mixture produced the best blasting agent known at that time. Alfred named it dynamite, and it revolutionized tunnel and canal building, the mining industry, and countless other operations.

Patents for dynamite were obtained in many countries, and manufacturing plants spread around the world. Alfred saw his enterprises grow into an international business, one that made him a millionaire many times over. A gifted financier, he concentrated all his energies on managing his affairs. He gave generously to many worthwhile projects, often helping young people by financing their education.

Although he was cultured and cosmopolitan with a wry

sense of humor, Alfred did not attend the parties, banquets, and receptions other well-to-do men enjoyed. In fact, he avoided any display of his wealth and social position. Always worried about his health—he had suffered from various illnesses since he was a child—he kept mostly to himself. When he traveled from nation to nation, he was melancholy and often lonely, without a true home.

In his forties he set himself up in a house and laboratory on an elegant street in Paris. Needing a secretary and household supervisor, he placed an advertisement for the job in a newspaper. Bertha Kinsky, the woman who answered the ad, was the daughter of an Austrian countess. But her family had lost its riches and she had found a position as a governess with the wealthy von Suttner family. Then Bertha had fallen in love with the von Suttners' eldest child, twenty-three-year-old Artur. Artur's parents, a baron and baroness, felt she was not a suitable match for their son and encouraged her to leave their home. At the time, then, Bertha had good reason to take an interest in Alfred's advertisement.

After an exchange of letters, Bertha traveled to Paris to meet Alfred. They got along well. Bertha later recalled he had a dark beard, was shorter than average, and had kind blue eyes. Alfred was impressed with Bertha's command of French and English and found her a refined and beautiful woman.

Many people feel she might have become his wife, but a few days after they met Alfred was called away to Sweden where a new Nobel factory was opening. While he was away, Bertha received a letter from Artur von Suttner. Before Alfred returned she had left Paris, married Artur in secret, and begun a new life.

Nevertheless, Bertha and Alfred maintained a lifelong friendship. They corresponded and, eventually, Bertha and

her husband met Nobel again. Later in her life Bertha became
a pioneer in the world peace movement and a famous writer.
Her novel, *Lay Down Your Arms*, revealed the horrors of war
and became an instant best-seller. Already interested in
promoting peace, Alfred's friendship with Bertha made him
even more aware of how much he wanted to encourage
positive instead of destructive world forces.

Throughout Alfred's later years he continued working
and traveling. He was devoted to his mother and made sure
she lived in beautiful surroundings. Eventually she and his
two older brothers passed away. For many years Alfred had a
love affair with an Austrian woman who was much younger
than he was. This relationship never gave him any real happiness, though, because she had little in common with him. As
he grew old, he was more alone than ever.

After suffering chest pains Alfred went to a heart specialist. The doctor prescribed a medicine which, although called
by another name, was made from nitroglycerine. Always
ready to laugh at himself, Alfred found it amusing that his
medication contained the very substance from which he had
made his famous explosives.

His private diaries and letters show he continued to use
his inventive and vigorous mind while his body grew weaker.
He died in a house he owned in Italy on December 10, 1896,
alone except for his servants. Bertha von Suttner learned of
his death by reading a newspaper account.

A year before he died, Alfred wrote a will that disposed of
his fortune in a way that surprised everyone. There was no
way she could have known at the time of his death, but—
because of the contents of this will—Bertha would receive an
unexpected honor nine years later. In 1905 she became the
first woman to win the Nobel Peace Prize.

Nobel's Will

Nobel distrusted lawyers, and he drew up his will without legal advice. When the will was opened after his death, however, lawyers all over Europe made up for lost business. For the will's contents set off an explosion different than but equal to any achieved by the inventor of dynamite during his lifetime. Through the wording of the will, which replaced two previous ones, Nobel sought to use his fortune to establish a series of prizes. Every year one prize was to be given in each of five fields: physics, chemistry, physiology (a branch of biology) or medicine, literature, and peace. The ambitious proposal, however, nearly remained nothing but words on paper.

In order for the prizes to be given, Nobel's share of the family's holdings had to be sold and the money put in funds that would produce income each year. His relatives felt that, should this happen, they would lose their rightful inheritance. They began to contest the will and argue about how they would divide Nobel's riches. Certainly there was enough for all—his estate was about $9 million at the time of his death.

Other problems soon arose. Since Nobel had lived and owned properties in many European countries, it was unclear where his legal residence had been. This decision, in turn, would play a large role in determining where the will was carried out and how it was interpreted. After many months the courts decided in favor of Sweden.

Objections kept coming. Why had Nobel decided four of the prizes were to be awarded by Swedish institutions while winners of one prize—the Peace Prize—were to be selected by the Norwegian parliament? No one was sure. Norway had been joined with Sweden in a United Kingdom for more than eighty years. But it had been an uneasy union and Norway, for all practical purposes, was self-governing. When Nobel died, demands for Norwegian independence were at their height. Many Swedes thought all the winners should be chosen by people from their country since Nobel had been a Swedish citizen. The Norwegian parliament, however, considered it an honor to have been selected and quickly chose a committee to oversee the selection process.

Nobel, it seemed, had aroused everyone. Even the king of Sweden and Norway, Oscar II, had some doubts about the arrangements. It took more than three years, but, finally, the problems were resolved. Mostly due to the efforts of one young man, Ragnar Sohlman, an assistant Nobel had particularly liked and trusted, the first prizes were awarded in 1901. As one of two executors of the will, Sohlman enlisted the help of Emanuel, Nobel's nephew and the head of the Russian branch of the family. Emanuel agreed to honor his uncle's desires and helped smooth over the differences among the Nobel relatives.

Quarrels ended, and the estate was settled. At last, according to Nobel's instructions, his fortune was used to establish a fund "the interest on which shall be annually distributed in the form of prizes to those who. . .shall have conferred the greatest benefit on mankind." Each prize was to be of equal cash value. The Nobel Foundation was set up to direct the fund, and the various institutions named in the will agreed to take responsibility for awarding the prizes. It was decided, as Nobel had wished, that winners would be chosen without regard to their country of origin.

The Prizes

Today, the Nobel Foundation, an organization independent of any government, continues to direct the fund and other properties. The interest earned is distributed to the

Nobel winners. Over the years the prize money has grown, but the exact amount changes from year to year. (Currently it is about $200,000.) While the union between Sweden and Norway was peacefully ended in 1905, Nobel's desire was respected, and Norway continues to award the Peace Prize.

A prize may be awarded to one, two, or three people. The sharing of a prize in no way lessens the honor. Other rules governing the awards say that a person must be living at the time an award is announced in order to win and that the Peace Prize and only this prize may be won by an organization as well as an individual. In addition, a prize does not have to be given each year in every field.

The Nobel Institutions

There are five special Nobel committees, one for each prize-awarding institution. Each of these committees has five members, and each may call upon outside experts for advice.

Prizes	*Prize-awarding institutions*
Physics	Royal Academy of Sciences
Chemistry	Royal Academy of Sciences
Physiology or Medicine	Nobel Assembly of Karolinska Institute
Literature	Swedish Academy
Peace	Norwegian Nobel committee with members appointed by the Norwegian parliament

A New Prize

In 1968, in observance of the three-hundredth anniversary of its founding, the Bank of Sweden established the Alfred Nobel Memorial Prize in Economic Science. The bank donated an annual amount to the Nobel Foundation for a prize to be awarded by the Swedish Royal Academy of Sciences. The same rules apply for this award as for the other five prizes. The Economics Prize was first awarded in 1969.

Selection Process

Only certain people can suggest candidates for Nobel Prizes. These include previous Nobel winners, members of the prize-awarding institutions and Nobel committees, professors at specific universities or those invited to do so, and individuals of certain organizations. No one can submit his or her own name as a candidate.

By February 1 of each year the Nobel committee must receive all the candidates' names. Then the committees submit reports and recommendations to their respective prize-awarding institutions. These groups make the final decisions after the candidates' merits are discussed. All of the proceedings, including the voting, are supposed to be kept secret.

The announcements of the winners must be made by the middle of November, although they usually occur during October. In recent years many American winners have learned of their selection when they answer a phone in the darkness of their bedrooms. Reporters in Sweden find out the news and place trans-atlantic calls, hoping they will be the first to obtain an interview. Because of the time difference between Sweden and the United States, the reporters are already at work while the Nobel winners are asleep. Official notice comes hours later via cable.

Presentation Ceremonies

The Nobel Prizes in physics, chemistry, physiology or medicine, literature, and economics are presented to the winners at a ceremony in the Stockholm Concert Hall on December 10, the anniversary of Nobel's death. The Peace Prize presentation takes place on the same day at the University of Oslo in Norway. In Stockholm the awards are given by the king, and in both cities the royal families attend the ceremonies. Each winner receives a Nobel gold medal, an individually designed diploma, and a check.

Nobel Week

Nobel winners are known as laureates, an honorary title that has its origins in ancient days when wreaths made from laurel leaves were placed on the heads of those who won important victories. Through the ages victors have been honored with feasting and merriment, and Nobel winners are no exception.

While December 10 is a highlight, the celebration really lasts for about a week. A winner's only official obligation is to present a lecture. This lecture can be on any subject, but most are related to a winner's work. Banquets, dances, receptions, and other festivities make many laureates feel they are in the center of a whirlwind. News coverage is intense, and winners usually give several press conferences. In spite of the hectic pace, they remember it as the most exciting time of their lives.

Nobel week takes place during the deep darkness of the Nordic winter. In Stockholm, for instance, the sun only peeks above the horizon for a few hours each day. Long before the first Nobel Prize was awarded, this was a season when light took on a special meaning. After the Nobel Prizes were established, some ancient observances became interwoven with the new celebration.

Candles, bonfires, and torchlight parades symbolize the belief that cold and night cannot last but will be banished by the returning warmth of the sun as the days gradually length-en. In one traditional pageant, a young girl representing Saint Lucia wears a crown of lighted candles and a long white robe. She and seven other candle-bearing young women serenade the Nobel winners in their hotel rooms early on the morning of December 13.

Criticisms

The prizes have been given for more than eighty years and have aroused some criticism. In their attempt to carry out Nobel's intentions, those who choose the winners have awarded prizes to people who were not considered by others in their field to be as qualified as candidates who were passed over. For example, such well-known writers as James Joyce, Marcel Proust, and Virginia Woolf did not win the Literature Prize. In addition, some critics feel Nobel intended the prizes to go to young people for whom the recognition and money would bring many years of fruitful work. But a good many of the awards have gone to those who already have completed their most important achievements. For these people the Nobel ceremony comes as the crowning point of a distin-guished career. Then, too, as scientific advances have become team efforts instead of individual investigations, it has be-come difficult to single out one, two, or even three people as laureates.

These and other objections are raised each fall when the awards are announced. But all of us realize how difficult it is to make perfect decisions, whether we are acting alone or as part of a group. The list of Nobel winners represents many of the top minds and talents of this century. On occasion, one of the awards has lifted a little-known researcher into promi-nence overnight. No other prize brings as much honor.

1.

Nelly Sachs

Literature Prize 1966

The plane climbed steeply, heading for Sweden. Two women on board knew they were lucky to be escaping from wartime Germany. Even so, Nelly Sachs and her mother were frightened because family, friends, and homeland would soon be far away. The women could take only two small suitcases with them on their dangerous journey. They had little money and neither spoke a word of the language they would hear when the plane landed.

But Nelly was taking with her something that was to prove more valuable than anything she could pack in a suitcase.

"Liebchen," she said, turning to her elderly mother, "my love of words is all I have left."

Just a few days before, Nelly had received a precious document allowing the Sachs to slip out of the circle of danger closing in around them. As Jews they were marked for death by Hitler, leader of the German government. One by one their relatives and friends had disappeared. Nelly knew they had been taken to concentration camps. It was in these places of terror that millions of Jews and other people were dying and suffering.

Nelly and her mother had already been ordered to report to such a camp when they learned they could escape to Sweden. As she was preparing to leave Germany for the flight that would take her to safety, Nelly found a way to laugh in spite of her fear. She stood quietly for a moment looking at the two pieces of paper—the document promising freedom, and the order to report to an almost certain death.

"I'm carrying life in one hand and death in the other," she said. "I hope I don't forget which paper to give the airport officials!"

A Sheltered, Comfortable Life

Nothing in Nelly's early life had given her reason to think she would ever be forced from her family's beautiful large home in the Tiergarten, the most fashionable neighborhood of Berlin. Expensive furniture filled the high-ceilinged rooms, and every day fresh flowers were placed throughout the house. When Nelly was born in 1891, her mother, Margareta, was only twenty. William, her father, was a well-to-do manufacturer and inventor.

Nelly was her parents' delight. When her father was at work, Nelly, who had no sisters or brothers to play with, would go into his large library and read for many hours. Some of the stories she found were fairy tales written by German authors about long ago romantic times. Other books mentioned the mysterious legends and beliefs of people who lived in Asian countries.

One day, when she was small, her father began to play his piano. Putting down the book she was reading, Nelly listened. Then her slender, small-boned body began to move with the music, and soon she was dancing across the polished floor. On and on her father played while Nelly twirled and glided in and out of the shafts of sunlight coming through the large, open windows.

For many happy hours in the years that followed, Nelly and her father shared their love of music. Nelly decided she wanted to have a career as a dancer and took lessons from a well-known instructor. When she was nine, she became ill and left school. Private tutors were hired for her. As she grew stronger, Nelly went back to her regular classes.

A shy girl, Nelly and her family led a sheltered, comfortable life. Although they were Jewish, the Sachs thought of themselves more as Germans than Jews. They loved their country, supported their government, and were good citizens.

On Nelly's fifteenth birthday she ran downstairs to find presents at her place at the breakfast table. By an odd twist of fate, one of the packages was to help save her life thirty-four years later.

The gift that was to be so important to Nelly was a book written by a famous Swedish woman, Selma Lagerlöf. In her novel, Lagerlöf described a magical world of imaginary creatures and the adventures of a hero named Gosta Berling. Nelly loved the story so much that she wrote to Lagerlöf, and the novelist answered. Soon they were writing frequently to each other.

When Nelly was eighteen, Lagerlöf received the Nobel Prize in literature, the first woman ever to achieve this honor. Because of their friendship, Lagerlöf was willing, many years later, to help rescue Nelly and her mother from Germany.

But now, as a teenager, Nelly had no worries about the future. Since she had always liked reading, she decided to see if she had any talent for writing. About the time she received Lagerlöf's book, she began a collection of stories describing people who lived many centuries before, in the Middle Ages. Nelly also had a marionette theater, about the size of a dollhouse, and she made up plays and gave performances for her family. At seventeen she decided she would rather write poetry than dance.

Nelly's first poems were about the birds, flowers, and small animals she saw in Berlin parks. Some of the imaginary places and people she read about in her father's library also became part of her poems.

The year Nelly was finishing high school, the Sachs decided to spend their vacation at a spa. Spas were popular resorts with fashionable hotels where families relaxed near clean, sparkling streams. Sometimes people who were sick came to drink the water, believing it would make them well again.

At the spa Nelly met and fell in love with a man who was also on vacation. Just who this man was, how many times Nelly saw him, and whether they thought of marrying remains a mystery. She didn't talk about him, but he is part of the poetry she wrote later in life.

As Nelly was growing from a schoolgirl into a young woman, Berlin was becoming one of the most exciting and interesting cities in Europe. By the 1920s the city was known all over the world for its fine orchestra. Artists and writers filled the restaurants, and tickets for opera and ballet performances sold quickly. In nightclubs, performers wearing exotic costumes entertained audiences by staging elaborate shows. A young black American woman, Josephine

Baker, became an instant success when she came to Berlin in 1926. Baker's singing and dancing helped introduce German audiences to a new kind of music called jazz.

While all this activity swirled around them, the Sachs—mother, father, and daughter—remained a normal, respectable family, living quietly and contentedly. But a force that was to tear apart their comfortable, upper-class life already was beginning to make itself felt in Germany.

Hitler's Rise to Power

At the center of the events that would forever change the Sachs' lives and bring misery to millions of Jews throughout Europe was an ordinary looking man, Adolf Hitler. Born in Austria, Hitler, who was a poor student, had trouble choosing a career. For a while he had to paint and sell picture postcards so that he could afford food and a place to sleep.

Hitler came to live in Germany when he was in his twenties and eventually became a German citizen. He loved his adopted country, and believed Germany should become the most powerful nation in the world. Together with other people who had the same feelings, Hitler formed a political group, or party, that became known as the Nazis.

Then, beginning in 1929, the economy of Germany and other countries all over the world began to fall apart. Factories and offices didn't need as many workers. Many men and women lost their jobs, went to banks, and took out all their savings. Soon, many banks ran out of money and had to close. Families could not even buy food. Long lines formed for free soup and bread.

People worried about the future. Germans were just as frightened as everyone else, and they looked for someone to lead them out of their troubles. Hitler saw that this was a perfect time to try to take over the government of Germany.

In speeches, Hitler told each group of Germans whatever they most wanted to hear. It didn't bother him that many of the things he promised would never happen. Above all, Hitler tried to blame the people he disliked for what was happening in his country. "The Jews," he announced, "are poisoning Germany."

Most Germans didn't believe what Hitler was saying. However, in 1933 he achieved his first goal when he was appointed chancellor. Only the president, Hindenburg, now held a higher position.

Like a slow-spreading sickness, the beliefs of the Nazi party began to take hold in Germany. Even the Sachs family, living on their quiet tree-lined street, would soon learn of Hitler's plans. Some changes already had come to the household.

One afternoon when Nelly was out, her father, who had been ill for some time, suddenly became worse. When Nelly returned, she found that a doctor had been called. She held her sobbing mother while they waited for news. When the doctor appeared, he just shook his head. For the most dangerous years of their lives, Nelly and her mother would have only one another.

Nelly was still writing. In 1921 her first book, *Legends and Tales*, had been published. This book was dedicated to Selma Lagerlöf. Later, some of Nelly's poetry appeared in Berlin newspapers. Because she used rhymes and wrote about the things she saw in nature, Nelly's poetry was thought to be old-fashioned. The popular poets of the day didn't write about the real world, but tried to express their innermost feelings.

While Nelly was writing gentle, lyric poetry in her home in Berlin, Hitler, living in the same city, was extending his power. In 1934, after President Hindenburg died, Hitler became Führer, leader of Germany. Before they realized what was happening, the German people found themselves with few choices. The Nazis were ready to punish—even by beating and killing—anyone who opposed them.

A Living Nightmare

Just as a sled gathers speed as it travels down a snowy hill, events in Germany began to move faster and faster until no one could find a way to stop them. Secret police forces were created, one of which was known as the Gestapo. Under orders from the Führer, the police killed any political enemies that might have been able to take control of the government.

The Nazis passed new laws that gradually took away the rights of Jewish people. One day, as a show of strength, Nazi police kept anyone from entering the offices of Jewish lawyers and doctors or from buying anything in Jewish-owned stores. Several days later, Jews were told they couldn't hold government jobs. Finally, with the Nuremberg Laws, they learned they were no longer German citizens. Many Jewish people understood their situation could only grow more dangerous. Thousands left Germany, but many others stayed behind.

Nelly and Margareta were told they could no longer live in their beautiful house. Like other Jews, they had to move to a less fashionable section of Berlin. Into the few rooms of their new home, a small apartment, they tried to fit the possessions they loved most. Heavy wooden furniture took up much of the space. On the walls, delicate embroideries and paintings hung close together. Tabletops held china nicknacks and pieces of old silver.

Determined not to give up all of their old way of life, Nelly still bought her favorite flowers, pansies. On holidays she made stollen, a special bread with raisins, cherries, and nuts.

Nelly's mother was now quite frail and unwell. Since Nelly didn't want to leave her alone, several good friends often came to visit. One day Nelly opened the door and welcomed one of these women. In her long dress with its white collar, Nelly reminded her friend of someone who might have lived during the romantic times of the past century. Around her neck, on a velvet ribbon, she wore a small jewel, and she still had the same dark curls she had as a girl.

"Tell me what you've been writing," Nelly said as soon as her friend, who was also a poet, had entered. "I can't wait to show you what I've done!" By concentrating on her work, Nelly was able to forget what was happening in her beloved homeland.

Because German Jews were so loyal to their country, they found it hard to believe their own government could turn against them. Finally, the events of a fall night in 1938 shocked even those who had clung to the hope that somehow the Nazi threat would vanish.

On this night, according to a carefully drawn-up plan, Jewish shops, homes, and synagogues were destroyed all over Germany. Many Jews were killed. The next morning the shining glass from thousands of broken windows littered the streets, giving this time of terror its name—Crystal Night. There was no longer any doubt of Hitler's intentions.

The Führer already had made progress in his campaign

to dominate other nations. After taking over Austria and Czechoslovakia, German armies invaded Poland. This invasion marked the beginning of World War II, a conflict that was to involve the most powerful countries on earth.

Nelly became more frightened and seldom left the apartment. She turned for comfort to her books, the only unchanging things in a world that was becoming more like a nightmare every day. The authors of some of Nelly's books wrote about the Bible. Others discussed traditional Jewish beliefs. Nelly often sat for hours lost in thought about these mysteries.

A Flight for Freedom

In 1940 the Sachs' life, as they had known it, came to an end. As their family and friends were forced into concentration camps, Nelly made a desperate effort to escape. If the Swedish government would grant them a permit to come to Stockholm, the capital of Sweden, Nelly and her mother could leave Germany. But thousands of other Jews also were trying to flee, and Sweden couldn't shelter all of them.

Selma Lagerlöf, the Swedish author Nelly had written to for many years, now helped save the Sachs' lives. One of Nelly's friends, Gudrun Harlan, was able to leave Germany because she wasn't Jewish. Gudrun went from Berlin to Sweden to see Lagerlöf. She didn't know that Lagerlöf, who was more than ninety years old, often couldn't recognize the people around her.

When Gudrun arrived in Sweden, she rushed to Lagerlöf's home, but the old woman's nurses and servants tried to keep her from entering. Pushing past them she saw Lagerlöf, wrapped in shawls, sitting in her living room. Gudrun knelt beside the famous author and told her about the Sachs.

"Please, Miss Lagerlöf," she begged, "won't you do something to help Nelly?"

"I don't know...I'm not sure," Lagerlöf said slowly.

In desperation Gudrun gave Lagerlöf a piece of paper and a pen.

"Just write your name here," she pleaded.

Lagerlöf realized that someone she loved was in great need. Struggling to control her hand, the tall frail woman managed to sign her name.

Gudrun took this paper, went to Prince Eugene, the brother of the King of Sweden, and asked for permission for the Sachs to come to his country. Because he was sympathetic to the troubles of the Jewish people, and because Lagerlöf was a famous Nobel Prize winner, Prince Eugene helped get the permit the Sachs needed.

In Berlin, Nelly and her mother anxiously waited for the document that could save them. The order to report to the concentration camp had come, and they were terrified. With only a few days left, the permit finally arrived. On their flight to freedom, Nelly realized she was a homeless woman, almost fifty years old. As the lights of Stockholm shone beneath the plane, Nelly had never felt more alone.

Refuge in a New Land

When the Sachs first arrived in Stockholm, they stayed in a refuge home for people who had fled the Nazi terror. Nelly was so small she slept in a child's bed. Then, with help from Swedish officials, Nelly and Margareta moved to a tiny apartment. Before Nelly could meet her old Swedish friend, Selma Lagerlöf died.

With hardly any money or friends, the Sachs had to begin their life over again. Nelly quickly learned Swedish and began to translate the writings of Swedish authors into German. Her work gave the Sachs just barely enough money to live. In the cold days of Stockholm, Nelly didn't even have warm gloves to wear.

From the safety of Sweden, Nelly read and heard about what was happening in Europe. Hitler humiliated Jews in every way he could. All Jews were forced to wear the yellow Star of David, symbol of their religion, so that they could be identified easily. Each Jewish man and woman had to take a new middle name, "Sarah" for women and "Israel" for men. Secret police came for Jews, herded them like cattle into trains, and took them to concentration camps. Many died from starvation and sickness. The Nazis separated those who could work from those who couldn't. The young, the sick, and the elderly often were killed immediately.

In some camps prisoners were told they could clean themselves in showers. Sometimes they were even given bars of soap to make them believe this story. Then Nazi guards pushed as many people as possible into buildings from which there was no escape. Poison gas was released into the buildings and whole families—men, women, and children—died in a matter of minutes.

During these years, only one out of every three European Jews managed to stay alive. The man Nelly had met when she was young, whom she had never stopped loving, was one of those who was killed in a concentration camp. He was forced to carry heavy stones until he collapsed.

A Writer Reborn
While thinking of these horrors, Nelly started writing again. Now, however, her poetry was nothing like what she used to write in Berlin. This new poetry, which didn't

rhyme, told about the sufferings of the Jewish people. Almost overnight Nelly seemed to become another person. She showed a fresh strength and a strong belief in her Jewish heritage. Many nights, not wanting to disturb her invalid mother's sleep by lighting a lamp, Nelly wrote in the darkness of their one-room apartment.

"My dear," said a new friend one day, "how do you manage to turn out anything on that machine?" The friend pointed to a delicate white typewriter that looked as if it would fall apart at the slightest touch. Each morning Nelly would type what she had handwritten the night before. It was hard to believe that from this dainty typewriter came poems that were cries of pain and sorrow.

Throughout history, the Jewish people had often been forced into exile, just as Nelly had fled to Sweden. Even in ancient times, divided into the tribes of Israel, they wandered for years without a homeland. Nelly realized that what was happening to her people in the Second World War was only one link in a long chain of events. One of her most powerful poems, "O The Chimneys," describes how Nazis burned the bodies of Jews killed in concentration camps.

> O you chimneys
> O you fingers,
> And Israel's body as smoke through the air.

Although Nelly could imagine herself behind the barbed-wire fences of the camps, no hatred or idea of revenge appeared in her poetry. Rather, Nelly's writings describe a circle of death and rebirth—how, from the ashes of destruction, new life will arise.

She named one of her collections *Death Still Celebrates*

Life. A poem from this collection shows how she felt:

> I do not know the room
> where exiled love
> lays down its victory
> and the growing into the reality
> of visions begins
> nor where the smile of the child
> who was thrown as in play
> into the playing flames is preserved
> but I know that this is the food
> from which earth with beating heart
> ignites the music of her stars—

Butterflies, sand, and other natural things appeared in Nelly's poems. She used these images to show that, in the real world, nothing lasts forever. In a few lines she often captured something that had caught her eye.

And a dragonfly's flimsy luck
above the rim of a well. ("Chorus of the Shadows")

But for the homeless all ways wither
like cut flowers. ("World, do not ask those snatched from death")

Behind the dusk
music of blackbirds. ("Oblivion! Skin")

Earth, old man of the planets, you suck at my foot
which wants to fly,
. . .

as you turn and turn
in your place among the stars,
beggar of the Milky Way
with the wind as guide-dog.
("Earth, old man of the planets")

Nelly's writings began to show her faith that the Jewish people would not be totally destroyed. She used the theme of new life in a play she wrote called *Eli*. Written in the form of a long poem, this play tells the story of an eight-year-old boy, Eli, who calls to God by playing on his flute as his parents are taken away by soldiers. Because one of the soldiers thinks the flute song is a secret signal, he kills Eli, and the boy's village is destroyed. Although death is a part of the story, the play is about beginnings. The people of Eli's village build new homes after the soldiers leave, and a broken fountain is repaired so that it once again fills with water.

Some of Nelly's Swedish friends published 200 copies of *Eli*. A few of these volumes found their way to Germany where the play was produced over the radio. Later it was given a stage production and made into an opera. While the poetry Nelly wrote after coming to Sweden also was being published, *Eli* made her well known.

As World War II ended, the German language, once used by the Nazis for evil purposes, came alive again. Since, in exile, Nelly had continued to write in a pure form of German, she was seen as a protector of her language.

After her mother died in 1950, Nelly lived alone in her Stockholm apartment. Her living room had a small glass sunporch overlooking the street. Nelly liked to sit there and watch cars and people pass by. Sometimes, because she thought so often of the suffering of her people, she imagined a group of terrorists was trying to harm her.

"Doctor," she once said to the understanding physician caring for her, "today they came after me when I was my car." Every so often her doctor would suggest she stay in a hospital until she became herself again. No hint of her own troubles, however, appeared in her writing.

Prizes for an Important Poet

With the publication of her fourth volume of poetry in 1958, Nelly Sachs began to be recognized as an important poet. The German people—especially those who knew and loved books—were the first to honor her. In 1960 Germans awarded Nelly the Droste-Hulshoff poetry prize. When she returned to her homeland to accept this honor, it was the first time in twenty years that she had been in Germany.

The next year the German city of Dortmund established a literature prize in Nelly's name. Famous authors wrote articles about her for a Festschrift, a book praising her work.

As she received more awards, Nelly continued to live quietly in Stockholm, seeing only a few friends. After describing the horrors of the holocaust, or destruction by fire of the Jewish people, Nelly's poetry changed again. What had happened in the war, she thought, was part of a larger plan.

Nelly believed that, just as all things on earth are constantly changing, men and women also are moving along a path toward some other way of life. The idea that all human beings are seeking a world of understanding and peace became a part of her writings. Because she was generous and did not believe Germans should be punished for what they had done, her poetry was read eagerly by those who wanted to recover from their war wounds—wounds of the mind as well as those of the body.

Nelly was awarded the Peace Prize of the German Booksellers' Association. In accepting this prize she gave young Germans a message: "In spite of all the horror of the past, I believe in you. Together . . . let us walk together into the future to seek . . . a new beginning."

Authors from many different countries became interested in Nelly and began corresponding with her. Young writers, especially Germans, came to see her in Stockholm.

In October of 1966, people passing Nelly's building saw a strange sight. Dozens of reporters formed a long line waiting to enter her small apartment. After spending many years alone, sometimes ill and with little money, Nelly had become an overnight celebrity. She had won the Nobel Prize in literature for her poetry. Sharing the prize with her that year was another Jewish writer, Shmuel Agnon.

In her apartment, amid bouquets of flowers from well-wishers, and offering glasses of wine to journalists, Nelly moved with the same graceful walk she had as a girl. Because she was used to talking for only a few minutes at a time, those interviewing her waited as she chose each word carefully.

That December Nelly and other Nobel winners came to the Concert Hall in Stockhom to receive their awards. Since, in recent years, Nelly had never been able to afford many clothes, she decided to buy a special dress to wear for the Nobel ceremony. "It's cornflower blue," she wrote to a friend, "and made of very heavy silk. I never thought I would have such a gown."

Nelly and Shmuel Agnon won the hearts of the distinguished guests and members of the Swedish royal family. Since both were short, the other Nobel winners towered above them. When Nelly received her prize, King Gustaf of

Sweden had to bend in half to reach down to her. Nelly curtsied, a gentle look on her face. Neither of the literature winners was young. Agnon was seventy-eight, and the day of the awards, December 10, was Nelly's seventy-fifth birthday. She didn't remind anyone, though, because she didn't want to make a fuss.

That same night there was a gala dinner for the winners in the Stockhom Town Hall. Nelly was escorted to her table by the Swedish king. The following day there was another dinner, this time at the royal palace.

A Quiet Life of Courage

People who aren't used to being famous sometimes change after they win the Nobel Prize. But Nelly stayed the same. She returned to her apartment and continued to write. Four years after becoming a Nobel laureate, Nelly died as quietly as she had lived. Hers was the kind of courage that is easily overlooked. Yet, no matter how small and birdlike she seemed, her poetry was full of strength. She had become a voice for millions of people who would never have a chance to speak.

As she received the Nobel Prize, Nelly remembered how, as a girl in Berlin, she had loved reading ancient legends filled with magical creatures. As a woman, her real-life journeys, both the escape to Sweden and the mind-journeys of her poetry, had been more fabulous than she had ever dreamed possible.

"It seems to me," Nelly said in the short speech she made at the Nobel ceremonies, "that a fairy tale has come true."

2.

Rosalyn
S. Yalow

Physiology or Medicine Prize 1977

Rosalyn was sitting on the flat roof of the building next door to where her grandmother lived. On this hot summer's day when she was thirteen, it was a place where she could relax in a beach chair and take a sunbath or read. To get there, she had crawled out of a window in her grandmother's apartment which overlooked the rooftop.

In the Bronx, the part of New York City where Rosalyn lived, people who did not have backyards often used their roofs instead. At night, in the days before air conditioning, families might gather there to share cool drinks and exchange news. During the day, wash sometimes dried on lines strung far above the streets below. Or, as was the case for Rosalyn, a roof could be a private place.

Sometimes she would look across Walton Avenue toward the apartment building where she lived with her parents, Clara and Simon Sussman, and her brother, Alexander. She could not have guessed that even though she would live almost all her life in the Bronx, she was about to begin a journey that would make her famous. Her journey was going to take place in her mind as she became a scientist and found a revolutionary way to combine nuclear physics and medicine. And since she would grow up to be a courageous woman unafraid to speak out, her fame would also allow her to express opinions on issues outside the scientific world.

A Love of Learning

As a teenager, Rosalyn already had the most important tool she needed. She enjoyed learning. Even when she was too young to go to school, her neighborhood library had been one of her favorite places. Once she started public school, she earned excellent grades and was especially good at mathematics. Since neither of her parents had been able to go to school beyond the elementary grades, they were proud of her talents.

Rosalyn and other teenagers growing up in the Bronx in the 1930s saw America as a country where hard work and a free education could lead to a rewarding life. The Sussmans and many of their neighbors were Jews whose families had been in the United States for only a generation. They passed on to their sons and daughters a strong desire for success.

At what, Rosalyn wondered, could she succeed?

"I couldn't carry a tune, I couldn't draw, I was a clod at dancing school, and I wasn't an athlete," she remembers about being a teenager. "So you could say I went into science because I loved it or because I wasn't very good at anything else."

At Walton High, an all-girls' public school, Rosalyn and her friends had strict but enthusiastic teachers. One in particular, a chemistry teacher, encouraged her interest in science. There was a difference, however, between Rosalyn and the other girls. "We all wanted to become big-deal scientists," she recalls, "but when I asked my friends if they were going to get married they said, 'no.' They must have been thinking of our teachers who were old maids. I told my friends I was going to be a scientist, get married, *and* have children."

Not many girls growing up in Rosalyn's generation expected to have both a career and a family. Yet she was determined and—as her family already knew—what she wanted to happen usually did.

After graduating from high school Rosalyn entered Hunter College, which was an all-women's New York City college. It was tuition free, which was important for Rosalyn because her parents could not afford to send her anywhere else.

She was happy at Hunter, where she majored in physics and chemistry and had the good fortune to be encouraged by her teachers. One day, when Rosalyn was a junior in college, she squeezed into a small classroom at Columbia University to hear Enrico Fermi talk. Fermi, an American physicist born in Italy, had recently won the Nobel Prize for his pioneering experiments with radioactivity.

Rosalyn saw that nuclear physics, the field in which Fermi and others were working, was one with a future for young scientists. When she received her degree from Hunter with high honors in 1941, she decided to go to graduate school. At the time, though, she found a closed door in her path.

"I was told that as a woman, I'd never get into graduate school in physics," she notes. "So, because I could type, I got a secretarial job at Columbia University's College of

Physicians and Surgeons. I had to promise to learn short-hand." After only a few months, however, the closed door opened. "I was admitted to the University of Illinois with a teaching assistantship and I tore up my shorthand books," she says with a grin.

When she arrived at the University of Illinois in 1941, Rosalyn discovered she was the only woman among 400 men on the junior faculty of the College of Engineering. She realized that the draft of young men into the armed forces, even before the United States entered World War II, had made available the university position she occupied.

Rosalyn did not have an easy time during her first year in graduate school. She had not had the same physics courses as the other students. To catch up, she had to take extra classes while she was also a half-time teaching assistant.

But school was not all work. On the first day Rosalyn met Aaron Yalow, another graduate student. Aaron, who was to become her husband two years later, would support and encourage her through the years to come.

When the Japanese attacked Pearl Harbor and America entered World War II three months after Rosalyn started graduate school, her physics department underwent many changes. Faculty members left to work on secret scientific work elsewhere. Young army and navy students filled the campus as they completed their training. For Rosalyn there was a heavy teaching load, graduate courses, work on her doctoral degree, and marriage in 1943.

She and Aaron set up housekeeping and grew accustomed to wartime life. To help supply materials for the war, America went on a rationing system. Coupon books were issued for such things as gasoline, butter, and shoes. When people wanted to buy something, they had to tear out a coupon and give it to a store's cashier along with the money for their purchase.

A Career and Family

In January 1945, Rosalyn received her Ph.D. in nuclear physics, but Aaron's degree was delayed. Soon the young couple made a difficult decision. Because the best place for two physicists to find work was in New York, Rosalyn would go to New York alone, get a job, and wait for Aaron to join her.

By this time Rosalyn—now Dr. Yalow—already had fulfilled a few of her early dreams. "I feel that during my life I've made a series of right decisions," she says. "I chose to concentrate on nuclear medicine, and I found a husband who understood and accepted the fact I wanted a successful career."

Sometimes a husband and wife can compete with each other, especially if both work in the same field. And yet, though both became physicists, Rosalyn and Aaron helped each other. "I've served as an extra pair of hands and eyes and another brain," Aaron notes. Rosalyn wanted to give Aaron all the things other wives gave their husbands. In their home, for instance, she was careful to observe the Jewish customs her husband cared about.

Rosalyn's life was fitting together like a jigsaw puzzle, even though some pieces were still not in place. Her student days were over, but what she had learned in school was just the beginning. "Getting a degree is only a first step in learning. What you need is much more than you can learn in school," she observes. "It almost doesn't matter what you study," she continues, "but what school really should

49

teach you is how to learn. The only thing is that you need a good background in math if you want to be a scientist."

When Rosalyn came to New York alone, she found a job as an assistant engineer at the Federal Telecommunications Laboratory. There she was the only woman engineer. The group she joined included Jewish engineers from France who had escaped before the German armed forces overran their country.

In September 1945, as World War II ended, Aaron received his doctorate, came to New York, and also found work. After living a short time in an apartment, the couple moved into a small house in the Bronx, not far from where Rosalyn had grown up. The group she was working for broke up when many of the engineers returned to France. When Hunter College, her former school, offered her a teaching position, she accepted.

A new home and a full-time job, in Rosalyn's words, "were hardly enough to occupy all of my time." Aaron introduced her to Dr. Edith Quimby, a leader in combining medicine and nuclear physics. Rosalyn volunteered to work part-time in Dr. Quimby's laboratory to gain experience.

Enrico Fermi, whom Rosalyn had heard speak when she was a Hunter College student, had built the first nuclear reactor in 1942. Nuclear reactors split atoms, releasing large amounts of energy. This development made possible, for the first time, the creation of large amounts of radioisotopes, the radioactive forms of substances known as chemical elements. Now that radioisotopes were more readily available, scientists were eager to learn how they could be used to identify and treat people with certain medical conditions.

As soon as she began to work for Dr. Quimby, Rosalyn

was taken to meet Dr. G. Failla, who was considered to be the top American medical physicist. Dr. Failla talked with Rosalyn for a while and then picked up the phone. Rosalyn heard him say, "Bernie, if you want to set up a radioisotope service, I have someone here you must hire."

Dr. Bernard Roswit at the Bronx Veterans Hospital was the person Dr. Failla had called. He followed Dr. Failla's advice and hired Rosalyn to work on his staff as a consultant. The Bronx hospital was operated by a government agency, the Veterans Administration (VA). It treated patients who had served in the U.S. armed forces and conducted important medical research.

On the December day in 1947 when Rosalyn started her work at the Bronx VA Hospital, she woke to find the streets covered with snow. Cars were so deeply covered that their owners had to dig them out with shovels. The weather forecasters were already calling the storm "the Great Blizzard of '47." When Rosalyn got to the hospital, she found that she had been given what used to be a large janitor's closet as an office. It wasn't a promising start, but that did not discourage her. While she was still teaching full-time at Hunter College, she equipped and developed the hospital's Radioisotope Service and began doing research projects with Dr. Roswit and other physicians.

In January 1950, Rosalyn decided to leave teaching and use all her energy in her work at the hospital. Then, that spring, something happened that would change her career. She met Solomon Berson, a young doctor who was finishing his training in medicine at the same hospital where she was working. When he joined the Radioisotope Service, he and Rosalyn began a twenty-two-year working partnership.

While Rosalyn's career was changing, so was her personal life. In the early 1950s, she and Aaron had two children—first a boy, Benjamin, and then a girl, Elanna. Less than ten days after giving birth to Ben, Rosalyn was back at work. "By the time Elanna was born," she remembers, "my doctors knew I'd try to go right back to work. So they kept me in the hospital for eight days. As soon as I got out, I went to Washington, D.C., to give a scientific talk."

Until Ben was nine the Yalows had a live-in helper so that Rosalyn could continue to work full time. As the children grew older, the family had part-time help. Sometimes Benjamin and Elanna took care of each other. Both parents enjoyed being with their children and found time to take them to movies and museums. On Sunday afternoons, when Rosalyn usually returned to the hospital to work, the children often went with her. There they played with the guinea pigs and other animals used for laboratory research. During these years the Yalows lived in a house in the Riverdale section of the Bronx, less than a mile from the VA hospital where Rosalyn and Sol Berson were making exciting disveries.

An Amazing Discovery

What Rosalyn and Sol were doing was detective work. A good detective team looks at the evidence, visits the "scene of the crime," collects clues, and comes up with a solution. The two investigators took their scientific knowledge—Rosalyn as a physicist and Sol as a physician—added many hours of laboratory work and a large dose of imagination. Then they made a discovery so surprising that, at first, hardly anyone believed their results.

This is what happened in their laboratory. For many years doctors had known that diabetics—people who have a disease known as diabetes—are unable to make normal use of a form of sugar known as glucose. They had also known that insulin, a hormone produced by the pancreas, a gland in the body, affects the way we use glucose.

Since the discovery of insulin thirty years earlier, millions of diabetics had been treated with insulin from animals. Rosalyn and Sol found that these people were developing antibodies to the animal insulin.

Antibodies, in a sense, are soldiers developed by our bodies to fight invading substances such as bacteria or viruses. The antibodies seek out and join with, for instance, a virus, and in doing so help destroy it. This is how we recover from such infections as the common cold.

Until Rosalyn and Sol's discovery, no one believed injected animal insulin would cause the formation of antibodies in humans. When the young scientists sent the results of their experiments to two well-known scholarly journals, *Science* and *The Journal of Clinical Investigation*, the editors of these magazines did not believe them. In fact, *Science* refused to publish their article and *The Journal of Clinical Investigation* only published it after the words "insulin antibody" were removed from the title. The two scientists also had to prove to the editors that they really had discovered an antibody.

In the course of this same work, Rosalyn and Sol found that they had a method that could measure the amount of insulin in a person's blood. Surprisingly, they found most adult diabetics had more than enough insulin. Some unknown factor was interfering with the action of insulin in their bodies. Even today no one has found the answer to this puzzle.

The technique that Rosalyn and Sol used to measure

amounts of insulin was called radioimmunoassay. To make it easier to talk about, it became known as RIA. RIA is not difficult to perform.

In a series of test tubes, a known amount of radioactive insulin is added to a known amount of antibodies against insulin. Then, to some of these test tubes, known amounts of insulin are added. To other tubes are added samples from blood that contain unknown amounts of insulin. By comparing how the radioactive insulin binds to the antibodies in both the tubes containing the known and unknown amounts of insulin, investigators can determine the amount of insulin in the blood samples.

The beauty of the RIA technique is that it allows accurate measurement of insulin in the blood at very small concentrations. In fact, one expert pointed out that measuring the amount of insulin in a test tube of blood is the same as showing that there is a teaspoon of sugar in a lake sixty-two miles long, sixty-two miles wide, and thirty feet deep.

The Perfect Collaborators

While Rosalyn and Sol's research was extraordinary, so was the way they worked together. Each person was an expert in a particular field, but each also wanted to learn from the other. It was this willingness that led Rosalyn, who had never studied biology in school, to become knowledgeable about medicine through Sol's teaching. Sol, who was, according to Rosalyn, "a natural mathematician," learned physics from her.

Two people who work together are called collaborators. For Rosalyn, at a crucial time in her career, Sol was the perfect collaborator. The two complemented each other in several ways. Rosalyn was seen as being very sharp-witted with a vigorous logical mind while Sol was something of a romantic with a mind given to flashes of insight. Most people who knew them when they worked together felt they accomplished more as a team than either would have separately.

For five years after doing their breakthrough research, Rosalyn and Sol hoped the RIA technique would be widely used. Members of the scientific community, however, were slow to grasp the technique's potential. This lack of acceptance did not stop the two researchers. If the technique could be used to measure the hormone insulin, couldn't it be used to measure other hormones? To find out, Rosalyn and Sol kept working. During the early 1960s, they learned that they could use RIA to find out if certain children are unusually small for their age because they have too little of a hormone that directs growth.

In fact, as Rosalyn and Sol were gradually learning, RIA could be used to measure almost any substance in the bloodstream as long as that substance produced—or could be made to produce—antibodies. Finally, after 1965, the scientific community began to realize what a marvelous tool the two Bronx researchers had given them. Instead of using existing measuring methods that sometimes required as much as a cup of blood, RIA could make more accurate measurements with just a few drops.

A Quiet Revolution

Once RIA's capabilities were realized, a revolution occurred. Other researchers began finding new ways to apply the technique. They discovered that a tiny sample of blood taken from infants at birth can indicate whether a condition called hypothyroidism is present. Hypothyroidism occurs when the thyroid gland is not normally active. If the condition is present, then immediate treatment can be begun. Without such treatment these infants' mental capacity would be below normal.

Along with another researcher, Dr. John Walsh, Rosalyn and Sol were successful in applying RIA to detect the hepatitis B virus that causes a disease which can severely damage the liver. Because of this development, RIA can be used to examine the blood in blood banks to ensure it does not contain this dangerous virus.

In other important developments, RIA made it possible to measure the levels of drugs circulating in the bloodstream. Such measurements help health professionals in two ways. First, doctors can monitor their patients and ensure that they do not receive a higher level of a drug than they need. Second, RIA can show whether or not people have given themselves or others illegal substances such as heroin.

Since RIA is not a difficult procedure to carry out, it was made available in kit form so that it could be used all over the world. "We did not patent RIA," Rosalyn says. "We made a scientific discovery and gave it to anyone who wanted to use it." It was a gift no one could put a price tag on.

As the years passed after Rosalyn and Sol had developed RIA, there was surprise each fall when the Nobel Prizes were announced and their names were not on the list. Rosalyn feels one of the reasons may be that she and Sol were both working in a VA hospital. Most people believed that high-quality research was not done at such facilities.

This situation changed in 1968 when Sol Berson left the

laboratory where he and Rosalyn had worked together for more than twenty years. He became the head of the department of medicine at Mount Sinai Hospital, also in New York City. Since he and Rosalyn remained collaborators, however, Sol's new job made them stand out more within the scientific community. At first Sol intended to keep working at the VA hospital several days a week, but he soon discovered his duties at Mount Sinai took up most of his time.

When the 1971 Nobel Prizes were awarded and they still had not won, Sol had no way of knowing he had lost his last chance. In April 1972, while attending a medical meeting in Atlantic City, New Jersey, he had a heart attack and died. According to Nobel's will, no one can receive a prize unless he or she is living at the time of the announcement.

Rosalyn was stunned. One of her first impulses was a generous gesture. At her request the laboratory they had shared was named The Solomon A. Berson Research Laboratory.

Carrying on Alone

When Sol died, many people thought Rosalyn would be unable to carry on alone. In a sense, she had to prove that during all the years she had worked with him, she had contributed her fair share to their research. Little did some observers realize that she had always had plenty of talent, self-confidence, and her own drive to achieve.

Rosalyn plunged back into her work, honoring all the commitments she and Sol had made before his death. Over the next five years she kept researching and won a dozen medical awards. In 1976 she became the first woman to win the Albert Lasker Basic Medical Research Award, an honor of which she was especially proud.

Then, one morning in the fall of 1977, Rosalyn was working at her desk at the laboratory. It was so early no one else was at work yet. Neither she nor Aaron had slept well as daylight came because it was the morning when the Nobel Prizes would be announced. There were reasons for her not to be too hopeful. No survivor of a scientific team had ever won, and, of the five women who had won Nobel Prizes in science, three had been married to their collaborators. Since they could not sleep, Aaron and Rosalyn had gotten dressed and gone to work. It seemed as if it would be an ordinary day. Rosalyn was usually at her desk by 7 A.M. anyway. But then the ring of the phone changed her day and her life.

The call was from Professor Luft, who headed a Nobel committee in Stockholm, Sweden. He told Rosalyn that she had won half of the Nobel Prize in physiology or medicine. The other half was to be shared by Dr. Andrew V. Schally of the New Orleans VA Hospital and Dr. Roger Guillemin of the Salk Institute in California. These researchers had used the RIA technique to make important discoveries about hormones in the brain. Rosalyn would receive half of the $145,000 prize money while Schally and Guillemin would share the other half.

It took a few moments for the message to sink in. Rosalyn was sitting only about fifteen minutes by car from her old childhood apartment building on Walton Avenue. Now the girl from the Bronx had grown up to win the prize all scientists want.

First Rosalyn called the hospital's chief of staff. Then Aaron called from the Cooper Union School of Engineering where he taught. He had heard the news and told Rosalyn, "You'd better go home and change your clothes. As soon as they hear what's happened, the photographers and reporters will descend on you." Rosalyn went home, changed, and was back at the hospital before eight.

In the few quiet moments before visitors came crowding into her office, she thought of what the award meant. Her joy was mixed with sadness. She wished two people could be alive—her father, who had died in 1959, and, of course, Sol Berson, with whom she would have shared the prize.

Then, quite suddenly, her office began to fill with people. Before giving a press conference, Rosalyn, who had already told the news to her son Ben, called her daughter Elanna, a graduate student in California. The rest of the day, Rosalyn says, "passed like a dream." Aaron and Ben came to celebrate at a hurriedly arranged party in the laboratory. As colleagues and friends swirled around her, she joked about what a good feeling it was to interrupt her work routine. When members of the press interviewed her, she made a point of thanking the Veterans Administration for their thirty-year support of her work.

The weeks from October, when the prizes were announced, until December, when they were awarded, were busy ones for Rosalyn. She gave talks she had promised to give, wrote several research papers in order to prepare new information for her Nobel lecture in Sweden, and carried on her regular lab tasks. On top of everything else, she flew to California just two days before leaving for Sweden with Aaron, Ben, and her mother to attend Elanna's wedding. Elanna and her husband decided to spend part of their honeymoon in Sweden so that they could watch Rosalyn receive her prize.

Also squeezed into her schedule was a different kind of

appointment. As she says, "Although I was famous for traveling all over the world to give lectures with just one small suitcase, I was quite willing to go to Stockholm with baggage appropriate for my new status as a Nobel winner." She always did things wholeheartedly if she did them at all, and her wardrobe was no exception. One of New York City's leading fashion designers offered to create a dress for her to wear when she received the prize. It was a deep blue chiffon with a brocade vest. Reporters were so interested in her activities that one newspaper carried a long article just about her dress!

A Busy Celebration

From the time the Yalow family flew to Stockholm, they became honored guests at events which seemed like a nonstop celebration. They held many press conferences, were chauffeured everywhere by limousine, and attended fancy dinners and cocktail parties. Three Bronx students— one each from Rosalyn's junior high school, Walton High, and Hunter College—came to Stockholm, too. The students attended many of the Nobel events and wrote about them for an American newspaper.

Finally the day of the Nobel ceremonies arrived. A crowd of about 1,800 people entered the Concert Hall where the presentations were made. Then came the Swedish royal family and, finally—as a mark of respect—the Nobel winners. As each winner rose to receive an award, a blare of trumpets echoed through the hall. When her name was announced, a radiant Rosalyn shook hands with the king, bowed to him and to the audience, and returned to her seat to watch Schally and Guillemin receive their awards. After the awards came the banquet at City Hall. Rosalyn was escorted into the banquet room by the king. Then, even later, came the celebration dance.

While the award ceremonies were the high spot of Rosalyn's Stockholm adventure, the Nobel lectures were a special event to remember, too. She was sorry that they were all given at the same time in different places in Stockholm because this prevented her from hearing the other winners speak. Her own Nobel lecture reported on work she had recently completed with Dr. Eugene Straus, a new collaborator. In the same lecture, she paid tribute to Sol Berson.

After the sparkle of Nobel week in Stockholm, it was time to come home. Things had changed, however. Rosalyn Yalow was, at fifty-six, the first American-trained woman to win a Nobel Prize in any of the sciences. Before winning the prize, she had been only one of many prominent researchers. Now she was a celebrity. If she wanted to say something—no matter what the subject—she was guaranteed an audience. Some Nobel winners do not like this kind of instant attention. Rosalyn, though, thrived on it.

Speaking Out

One of the issues Rosalyn wanted to speak out about is the public's misunderstanding about low-level radiation risks. As someone who has worked with radioactive materials for all of her career, she often says that disposing of radioactive wastes from medical laboratories does not present a danger to the community. She believes the radiation given off by most radioactive laboratory wastes is so low that the wastes can be disposed of as if they were non-radioactive.

Rosalyn points out that we all are continually exposed

to cosmic radiation from the sun, stars, and outer space. In fact, as she notes, all of our bodies contain a small amount of radioactivity. Her awareness of this fact once led to an interesting situation. A legislator introduced a bill saying there could be no radioactive materials transported along county roads in his jurisdiction. "I observed that then *he* wouldn't be able to drive to work," Rosalyn says, laughing with a glimmer of impatience in her eyes.

She also says that while the news media reports stories about the dangers of radiation, most people are not told that scientists know a great deal about the effects—or absence of effects—of low-level radiation. For instance, she points out that on the Colorado plateau in the United States, where the city of Denver is located, natural radiation levels from the high altitude and from the soil are twice what they are in New York State. Yet, according to the American Cancer Society, the cancer death rate in this area is less than in New York State.

While the Nobel Prize put her more in the spotlight, in some ways it did not affect Rosalyn at all. As usual, she often spent eighty to one hundred hours per week working in the laboratory. The excitement of doing experiments that might unlock more mysteries remained.

A few years after winning the Nobel Prize, Rosalyn and her staff moved into a new laboratory at the Bronx VA Hospital. This laboratory takes up an entire floor in a modern building. Rosalyn now has a private group of rooms, including an office, her own small laboratory, a conference area, and a room for her secretary. The main laboratory has space for many types of activities. It includes a "cold" room for materials that need low temperatures and a "hot" room for radioactive substances.

An important section of the laboratory contains guinea pigs, rabbits, and mice that are used in experiments such as those requiring the development of antibodies. The animals are taken care of by the staff on workdays, but on weekends and over vacations Rosalyn still cares for them herself as she always has. A laboratory assistant laughingly says that Rosalyn talks to the animals as she works with them. If, for example, a particular animal is not developing antibodies as hoped, Rosalyn might say, "Okay, shape up," and usually the animal responds by developing what is needed.

The laboratory is a busy place. In addition to the regular staff, there are always several doctors from other countries working on special projects. Rosalyn calls her research assistants "my professional children," and she makes sure there are not too many of them so that she can talk to each one every few days. While some scientists have been known to jealously guard their achievements, Rosalyn hopes those receiving training in her laboratory will eventually surpass what she has done. "Unless each generation does more than the last, the course of civilization will be downhill," she believes.

What is it like to work for Rosalyn? Violet Mallory, her longtime administrative assistant and secretary, says that her job is demanding. But it is made easier, she adds, because Rosalyn knows exactly what she wants. Then, too, Rosalyn's sense of humor and her variety of interests make it fun. "She's liable to go—in one conversation—from what she's going to buy in the supermarket on her way home to a discussion of people's fear of the biological effects of radiation," Mallory says.

Rosalyn herself does not find this unusual. "We've got to treat women as whole people," she says. "They can be wives, mothers, and successful professionals." Because she thinks women should compete with men in fields where they have an equal chance of doing well, she opposes the awarding of "women-only" prizes. Acting on this belief, in 1978 she refused to accept the Ladies' Home Journal Woman of the Year award.

Sometimes her staff teases her about how easily she combines her different responsibilities. When she wanted to celebrate after winning one award, she cooked several turkeys at home and brought them to the VA hospital where the party was to be held. "But she made the potato salad right in the lab while she was talking to us about a research project," one assistant remembers.

Because she believes young people should start early to think of what they want to do later on, Rosalyn often talks with junior high and high school students. When she went back to Walton High thirty-seven years after graduating, she told the audience, "You won't all win Nobel Prizes, but the important thing is that you set goals for yourself and then live up to them." After hearing her talk one student said, "What I like about her is that she encourages you to do what you enjoy most, not to try to imitate her."

Rosalyn does think that every high schooler, even those who do not want to become scientists, should have a one-year course in general science that combines biology, chemistry, and physics. That way, she believes, when these students can vote they will be more knowledgeable about such matters as pollution.

Once scientists become fascinated by detective work, they find it hard to stop their investigations. Rosalyn continues to try to put established facts and new research together to answer medical questions. Recently she has been doing studies on how antibodies affect the substances that pass from a pregnant woman across the placenta—the life cord connecting her with her unborn child. She has become Distinguished Professor-At-Large at Yeshiva University and head of the Department of Clinical Sciences at Montefiore Hospital. At the same time, she has continued in her position as Senior Medical Investigator at the Bronx VA Hospital.

"I'll never retire," she says, "even though there are lots of other things I'd like to try. Archaeology would be fun," she continues. "I guess we'd all like to start with places mentioned in the Bible. Or I'd go to dig up artifacts from the Incas and Aztecs."

Within her wide-ranging interests, she continues to hold a special place for Aaron and her children. Elanna is now a psychologist specializing in education, and Ben works with computer systems.

But, above all, Rosalyn has never stopped being curious. "The excitement of learning separates youth from old age," she says. "As long as you're learning you're not old." And it is that enthusiasm about wanting to know things that connects the young girl who sat on a Bronx rooftop one hot summer day with the woman for whom the Nobel Prize was simply another milestone—although a very meaningful one—along a continuing road.

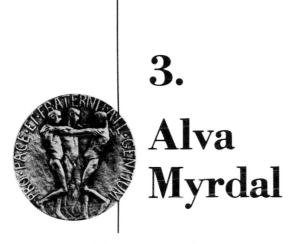

3.

Alva Myrdal

Peace Prize 1982

"I've always wanted to straighten things up," Alva Myrdal says. "When I was a young child, I saw a staircase with some missing parts and I asked, 'Why don't they fix the broken staircase?' " As she grew older, Alva kept on trying to change what she saw. But now she was working on a larger scale. First she helped alter social conditions in her homeland, Sweden, and then she took on the entire world as she worked for peace and disarmament.

Born in 1902, Alva was the oldest of five children of Albert and Lowa Reimer. Her father was a building contractor and her mother an excellent seamstress. At first the family lived in Stockholm, capital of Sweden, but, when Alva was still small, they moved to one of the city's suburbs.

As a young child, Alva often sat under her father's desk and listened to him talk about his work. At home she also listened to her parents' discussions about politics and daily events. Her father was a member of a political party known as the Social Democrats, while her mother had political views of her own. Her parents' exchange of ideas, Alva says, was an important influence in her early life.

With the coming of World War I, the family moved to a town called Eskilstuna. There Alva's father became a farmer. He also played a role in local affairs and served on the town council.

A Desire for Education

Although Alva does not speak often about her childhood, she does mention that she always loved to read. Her father had a small collection of books by such well-known writers as August Strindberg and Émile Zola. When Alva read novels by these authors, she became fascinated by the new, bold literary styles and ideas she found. The Reimer family discussed these ideas, and Alva says, "everyone had a different opinion."

Although she received high marks in school, Alva sometimes found her studies unexciting. As a teenager she found ways to learn what she wanted. Astronomy, for instance, she studied through a correspondence course. Pen pals were important, too. Through a Norwegian pen pal she became interested in Edvard Munch, an artist whose work revealed the emotions—particularly the anguish and terror—that are part of modern existence.

In the summer of 1916, Alva finished the eighth grade in her Eskilstuna school. Since the local high school was for boys only, she had no way to continue her education. Her only alternative was a one-year business course, which she decided to take. After completing the course she got a job working as a clerk in an office.

But Alva had no intention of spending her future as an office worker. She was determined to get a university education, and the only way she could enter Stockholm University was to pass a difficult examination—one that included questions in eleven different subjects. Her parents had different opinions about what Alva wanted to do. Her mother thought she was making a mistake. She wanted Alva to stay at home and not take the big step of going out into the world alone at such a young age. Her father, however, supported her. When she was seventeen, he made it possible for her to take private lessons with a few other girls.

Alva learned quickly and managed to pass the examination and become a university student. Even then she met with opposition. As she told her biographer, Lars Lindskog, "I wanted to become a doctor, but people said, 'She'll get married so why spend money on her' and they tried to give me as short a period of study as possible. I let them believe I wanted to become a librarian because that way I could study the subjects I was interested in." Alva took courses in world history, religion, and literature. Later, in her work, she drew on information she learned during her university years.

A Partner for Life

When Alva was seventeen and still living on her parents' farm, some students passing by on a bicycle vacation got permission from Alva's parents to spend the night in the Reimers' barn. In the morning Alva offered them coffee. One of the visitors, a young man named Gunnar Myrdal, decided right on the spot that he was going to see more of her. When the two met again, they plunged into discussions that jumped from one topic to another.

More than sixty-five years later, Alva and Gunnar are still having similar discussions. They were married one month before Alva received her bachelor's degree from Stockholm University in 1924. The intellectual give and take of their relationship has been a great influence on both their lives. As a couple, their wide-ranging interests always have attracted others.

The Myrdals' apartment became a meeting place for other young men and women, particularly those who wanted to talk about Sweden's social and political affairs. One friend from that time remembered that Alva always listened carefully to what the others had to say and did not do a great deal of talking. But, when she did contribute something, she spoke clearly and convincingly.

As Alva told Lars Lindskog, "I could not just stop learning [after receiving a university degree]. I wanted to continue my studies." She was particularly interested in psychology—the science of mind and behavior—and in philosophy and education. She decided to broaden her knowledge by reading books available only outside of Sweden. Alva and Gunnar traveled to several European countries. In a letter from London, Alva told a Swedish professor about the wonderful libraries she had found in that city.

An American Adventure

In 1929 the Myrdals received grants from the Laura Spelman Rockefeller Memorial Foundation to travel and study in the United States. This trip was a milestone for them both. Before coming to America, Alva was considering a career as a teacher and researcher. But the trip made her take a different path—one that would have a great impact on the lives of the Swedish people. Gunnar, on his way to becoming a university professor in economics, also was deeply affected by this trip.

The Myrdals came to America during an eventful and troubled time. Complex economic patterns set in motion years before came to a head during their voyage across the Atlantic. Within a few days of their arrival, the United States stock market "crashed." This event marked the beginning of a period of worldwide poverty and tragedy—the Great Depression.

As they compared Sweden with America, the Myrdals thought each country had some advantages and disadvantages over the other. It seemed to them that in the United States there was more of a striking contrast between the rich and the poor. They admired Americans' "frontier spirit" and freedom of expression. But they also thought it seemed difficult for U.S. citizens to make their ideas take the form of positive political action. In this regard the Myrdals thought Sweden offered the possibility of faster change for the public good. Sweden, for instance, had government-owned railroads and hospitals and, to the Myrdals' way of thinking, this arrangement made for a more efficient way of running things.

They also observed, however, that, as Alva put it, Sweden was "backward by comparison [with America] in many ways." She cited the Swedish teaching system, the courses taught in the schools, and the treatment of women as some aspects of Swedish life that needed improvement. "I found American women much more advanced than Swedish women," she recalled later on.

With their 1929 trip the Myrdals began an association with America that was to continue all their lives. From America they traveled to Geneva, Switzerland, for a year where they continued their studies.

Geneva was the headquarters for the League of Nations, an organization established after World War I to promote peace in the world. Alva and Gunnar had high hopes for this peacekeeping group. They found, however, that the League was not succeeding in its aim. The great world powers preferred to make their own decisions and, too, the League had some internal weaknesses.

The Myrdals decided to return to their homeland and see if they could help bring about changes in Swedish society. They believed that if people worked to improve their own countries, then, perhaps, nations would cooperate to make the world situation better.

Ideas for Reform

Back in Sweden in 1932, the Myrdals began the steps that would make them famous. Gunnar became professor of economics and financial science at Stockholm University. In addition, he began to work on several government commissions. Alva became an assistant at the psychological clinic at Sweden's main prison and worked toward her master's degree from Uppsala University. Most importantly, the Myrdals began writing a book that was to make them the most well-known Swedish couple of the 1930s.

Their book, *Crisis in the Population Question*, aroused widespread public interest. It had a direct influence on the social policies adopted by the Swedish government in coming years. These policies would make Sweden a forerunner among nations in offering its citizens cost-free government programs in such areas as health, child care, and housing.

Crisis in the Population Question appeared in 1934. In the same year Alva received her master's degree and gave birth to a daughter, Sissela. The Myrdals already had a son, Jan. In their book Alva and Gunnar noted that Sweden had the lowest birth rate of any country in the world. If this situation continued, they believed, the nation faced a bleak future. As its people grew older, the economy would lag and the nation would gradually grow weaker.

What was the reason for this fall in the birth rate? The Myrdals said it was caused by families in distress. Unemployment most strongly affected the same young workers who were most likely to be parents. Wages took no account of family responsibilities and housing was poor—especially for large families. In short, the Myrdals said that many would-be parents, faced with the choice between poverty with children or a higher standard of living without children, chose not to have children at all or not to have as many.

Skillfully, Alva and Gunnar used the population problem—already of concern to Swedes—as a springboard for social reforms. These reforms, they said, should come about through political action. Alva and Gunnar proposed that the government of Sweden take bold steps. They called for loans and allowances to encourage married couples to have children. They also wanted the government to provide medical care for pregnant women as well as cost-free health care and school lunches for all Swedish children. Mothers should be able to work after having children, the Myrdals believed. For this reason, well run day-care centers were an important part of their overall plan.

These suggestions aroused strong debate, but others brought about even greater controversy. The Myrdals proposed tax deductions for families with children and higher taxes on childless couples. Even more startling in the 1930s, they called for "sexual reforms" which included making information on birth control readily available and promoting sex education in the schools.

Alva, in particular, was criticized for her convictions. She concentrated on what many people then thought of as "men's issues." Some Swedes took the view that she should be busy with her duties as a mother of young children. Once, when she gave a talk, a male doctor in the audience stood up and said, "Why don't you go home and take care of your baby?"

But Alva believed in what she was doing. *Crisis in the Population Question* carried the right message to the right people at the right time. The Myrdals' suggestions struck a responsive note with other Swedes—particularly the young.

Alva and Gunnar had joined the Social Democratic party. Through this political group their reform ideas stood the best chance of success. When, in 1936, an election produced a decisive victory for this party, the stage was set for their ideas to become real programs. The following year, during a so-called "mothers and babies session," the Swedish parliament approved a great many of the proposals first set forth by the Myrdals in their 1934 book. Their ideas thus had a lasting effect on Swedish society. It was an impressive achievement, of which both Alva and Gunnar were proud.

Alva also had other accomplishments to her credit. In 1936 she founded and became principal of a school designed to train teachers in early childhood development and parent education techniques. The founding of this education center revealed a continuing concern on her part for the health and proper rearing of Swedish youth. In a book she wrote, *City Children*, Alva stressed the need for quality day-care centers. She was concerned with every detail of a child's development—even the design of toys.

During these years Alva also pushed for equal rights for

Swedish women. As a leader of the Women's Work Committee, she said Swedes should realize more and more women were going to have jobs. Society should adjust to this fact, she said, by providing flexible work schedules for mothers as well as for fathers. In a book she wrote with four other women, she stressed the importance of establishing a harmony between women's two roles: motherhood and productive work.

But books were not the only means of communicating her ideas. Through lectures and radio talks, she proposed additional changes in Swedish society. For instance, she said fathers should play a greater role in the daily lives of their children. In addition, together with Sven Markelius, an architect, she guided the construction of a city apartment house specially designed to serve the needs of working families. This high-rise building was placed in a parklike setting to provide fresh air and playing areas for children. The building contained private family units, a restaurant, office space, and a child-care center.

The Dangerous War Years

In 1938 the Myrdals once again decided to change the focus of their lives. As had happened in 1929, a trip to the United States figured in their plans. By now there was a "pause" in the reform efforts in Sweden. Growing disagreements among European countries, which would soon lead to World War II, were causing governments to spend more and more for military purposes. Alva and Gunnar felt they had done all they could for their homeland at this time.

When the Carnegie Foundation offered both husband and wife the chance to return to America, they accepted. Alva would study child psychology at Columbia University in New York City and also work on a book interpreting Swedish social programs for Americans. Gunnar would research race relations in the United States.

The Myrdals arrived in the United States in September 1938 with three children, for another daugher, Kaj, had been born in 1936. They also brought along two young women from Sweden to help run their household. The family settled near Columbia University where Alva took courses and researched her book. She enjoyed watching her children's progress at school: Jan, 11, at Horace Mann, Sissela, 4, in preschool, and Kaj, 2, in a nearby nursery school that met in a well-known landmark, The Riverside Church.

When Germany invaded Poland in September 1939, the Myrdals were still in America. Seven months later, in April 1940, Gunnar was in Washington, D.C., on business while Alva was in New York. She was scheduled to give a talk that night. Jan rushed into the living room of their apartment and said he had heard a news bulletin on the radio announcing the occupation of Norway and Denmark by the Germans. Alva went ahead and gave her talk and then met Gunnar in Washington to discuss the situation. Together they decided they should return to Sweden.

Friends tried to talk them into leaving their children in America, but Alva said, "If children in Sweden are exposed to the dangers of war then our children should be, too." Finding a way home was not easy. Finally the Myrdal family boarded a ship that was part of a convoy carrying planes and ammunition to Finland. Once they arrived in Finland, they saw the destructive power of war firsthand. While waiting for a plane to Sweden, Alva and Gunnar made a quick trip to Norway to see members of the Norwegian underground who were still resisting the Germans.

Arriving in Stockholm, they were disappointed because they were not offered official positions to help their country. Not long after, Gunnar returned to America. Alva remained in Sweden to work as principal of the teachers' training school she had founded earlier. In the summer of 1941, Alva decided to join her husband in the United States. She left their children in Sweden with Gunnar's mother, who came to stay in their home in Äppelviken, a suburb of Stockholm.

Alva's trip was quite an adventure. She was allowed to fly to England on a secret military flight because she promised to write articles on conditions in England for Swedish publications. (She lived up to her agreement and these articles eventually were gathered together and published as a book.) Then she had to remain in England for more than a month since there was no way to leave. "It was horrible," she says, remembering those days when the Germans were attacking the British. "If bombs fell in the night, I sat shivering with fright."

Finally she reached Lisbon, Portugal, where she waited another month and eventually managed to get on a plane going to America. Because one of the passengers on the plane weighed too much, Alva was given his seat. The plane made many stops before reaching the United States. Alva became part of a small group of passengers who stuck together during these days. The group came from all over the world, and Alva says she learned a great deal about world problems during their conversations.

This same year, 1941, the book Alva had written with support from the Carnegie Foundation was published. It was titled, *Nation and Family.* In it she explained the social reforms—in particular those affecting children and families—that the Myrdals had helped bring about in Sweden and called for them to be expanded.

By October of 1942 Alva and Gunnar had returned to Sweden. During World War II Sweden followed a policy of being armed but neutral and managed to avoid direct involvement in the war. The country became a haven for refugees fleeing Nazi-occupied nations. As more and more came, Alva became involved in work centered on helping these displaced people. With their needs in mind, she helped arrange for radio programs and magazines. She also served on a committee for international aid to war victims.

During the war years Alva and Gunnar's home became the center for intense discussions. People from Nazi-occupied countries came there to talk about restoring freedom and civilization once military victory had come to the Allied powers. Many who came were German-speaking refugees in exile. What made this group unusual was that quite a few members later became leaders of postwar Europe. For instance, Willy Brandt, who would become chancellor of West Germany, and Bruno Kreisky, who became Austrian chancellor, were among the Myrdals' visitors. Alva was very active in two subcommittees formed by this group—one on financial matters and the other on cultural affairs.

During these years Alva served as vice-president of the International Federation of Business and Professional Women. She also worked on changing Swedish school policies, and was elected a member of the Social Democratic Party's commission to develop postwar programs.

An International Couple

In the late 1940s, Alva and Gunnar's life became truly international. Gunnar accepted a job in Geneva, Switzerland, as head of the United Nations Economic Commission for Europe. Now the Myrdals centered their energies on bringing about world progress toward peace through the United Nations (UN), which replaced the League of Nations. Alva and the children accompanied Gunnar to Geneva and, in 1949, the United Nations offered Alva a job, too. She was asked to become director of the UN's Department of Social Affairs. When she accepted the job, it meant moving to New York and traveling back to Switzerland when she wanted to see her family.

The Myrdals managed for more than a year with jobs an ocean apart. Alva was the first woman to hold a high United Nations post and serve as a member of the UN Secretariat. She was not an unknown in international circles, however, for she already had been a member of several important postwar conferences. Her new area of work was large. It included directing projects in the fields of human rights, freedom of information, population questions, the status of women, and narcotics and drugs. Alva met prominent American women such as Eleanor Roosevelt and flew to Ecuador to help provide emergency relief for victims of an earthquake.

She was particularly enthusiastic about her department's program of technical training and assistance. Under this program people from one country could learn skills in another country. Then they returned home to organize projects for such groups as handicapped children. In addition, Alva established a process in her department whereby countries were put on a "black list"—those that had no voting rights for women, for instance—or on a "white list"—those that had made progress in directions encouraged by the UN.

Then, in the fall of 1950, Alva was offered the position of director of the Department of Social Sciences of UNESCO (the United Nations Educational, Scientific, and Cultural Organization). This specialized agency of the UN is headquartered in Paris, France. During the time her work had kept her in America, Alva had worried about her two teenage daughters. She believed they needed both parents nearby. When, in 1951, she accepted the UNESCO job offer, the desire to be nearer her family in Europe played a part in her decision.

UNESCO, which came into being in 1946, sought to remove social, religious, and racial tensions by encouraging the free exchange of ideas as well as cultural and scientific achievements. The improvement and expansion of educational opportunities also were UNESCO goals.

Alva stayed in her UNESCO job until 1955. Of those years she told Lars Lindskog, "We succeeded in doing a lot of things that people take for granted today." She says the international groups formed during the early 1950s set up a worldwide network of people who have continued to work for progress toward peace. She also takes pride in starting a social/scientific magazine through whose pages specialists in many countries could exchange information. During this time a fellow Swede, Dag Hammarskjöld, became secretary general of the United Nations.

The 1950s were a decade when Alva's career flourished. In addition to her UNESCO work, the government of Sweden appointed her ambassador to India and minister to Ceylon (1955-61) and minister to Burma (1955-58). During the time Alva was in India, Gunnar spent part of each year in that country gathering material for another book, *Asian Drama*.

When Alva became ambassador to India, there were those in the Swedish business community who expressed concern. They thought her political views would prevent her from promoting trade between the two countries. Within a short time, however, she became a close friend of Prime Minister Nehru, leader of India. She also won praise from her former critics by demonstrating a grasp of Indian affairs and an ability to deal with trade matters.

When Alva was almost sixty years old, she became a member of the Swedish parliament. A few years later she was named to the Swedish cabinet as minister in charge of disarmament and church affairs. Stopping the dangerous nuclear arms race had become her foremost concern in 1961, the year she returned to Sweden from India. At that time she was asked to become advisor on disarmament to the Swedish foreign minister. Before accepting, Alva researched the subject, became absorbed by its challenges, and eagerly accepted the job.

Working for Peace and Justice
Within a year she was named Sweden's representative to the United Nations Disarmament Committee in Geneva, a position she held until 1973. In Geneva, Alva became a spokesperson for the neutral countries—those that avoid taking the side of any of the superpowers. Under her guidance Sweden became a leader of this neutral grouping of nations. She also became president of the Dag Hammarskjöld Foundation, an organization devoted to continuing the efforts of the Swedish statesman and UN leader who was killed in a plane crash in 1961.

Throughout her career Alva always made sure she had the knowledge to back up the points she made. At the disarmament meetings other delegates, even those who disagreed with her, had to admit she was well prepared. She became an expert in the methods of nuclear warfare—including the scientific advances that made such warfare possible. Her understanding allowed her to make speeches that were praised for their sharp analysis of complex concepts. Her excellent command of English—a second language for most of the delegates—helped her put her points across in a readily understandable way.

Gradually, Alva became convinced that each of the two superpowers—the United States and Russia—were engaged in a struggle to, as she put it, "be second to none." In an extension of this view, she believed that "those who have power have no will to disarm." Alva presented her arguments in a book, *The Game of Disarmament: How The United States and Russia Run the Arms Race*, published in 1976. This book was hailed around the world. In America, for instance, its well organized, reasoned approach was praised. A reviewer for *The New York Times* said, "I cannot imagine a more significant book, whose theme is nothing less than a matter of life or death."

In *The Game of Disarmament*, Alva cut through diplomatic jargon and discussed, in plain language, specific events that took place in Geneva when she was there as a delegate. Her eyewitness accounts described the tactics she believed the superpowers used to delay the disarmament process. In addition to nuclear weapons, her comments covered chemical and biological warfare.

Throughout her career Alva never offered criticism without, at the same time, making suggestions for improvement. Therefore, in her book, she stressed the need for a world disarmament conference. She also recommended conditions the attending nations—the superpowers included—would have to agree to beforehand. The two important conditions would be a pledge not to be the nation to start any act of nuclear warfare and a pledge not to attack any nuclear-weapons-free country with nuclear weapons. She also made other specific suggestions that could lead to an international agreement.

Above all, Alva stressed that nuclear war *is* preventable. The people of the world, she wrote, must not give up their attempts to arrive at global cooperation by peaceful means. If nations decreased their defense budgets, she pointed out, they would have money to spend on health, education, and housing as well as other social needs. Scientists and engineers now engaged in research for military purposes could work, instead, on economic and social programs.

Over the years Alva's various positions brought her in contact with some of the most influential twentieth-century leaders. The long list includes Henry Kissinger, during the years before he became United States secretary of state. She also met Andrei Gromyko, the Soviet diplomat and foreign secretary, and Indira Gandhi, Nehru's daughter and an Indian leader in her own right.

But Alva's husband, Gunnar, remained the one with whom she shared her innermost thoughts. Their discussions began at the breakfast table as they read the daily newspapers and continued on and off all day. They worked at desks facing one another and frequently read each other's book manuscripts. Until recently, when both have been ill, the Myrdals often entertained. One friend remembers dinner parties with Alva and Gunnar where there was "never a dull moment."

The social reforms the Myrdals helped bring about

made Sweden the world's most advanced welfare state. Government- and business-supported programs sought to give Swedish women and men the chance to combine parenthood and career opportunities. Over the years, however, drawbacks in these programs emerged. Costs have risen, and taxes to pay for them are high. Sweden's experience reveals that planning for social benefits is a complex process that must be carefully achieved.

Prizes and Honors

Beginning quite early in their careers, the Myrdals won awards and honorary academic degrees. By the 1970s the recognition for their achievements was coming from organizations around the world. Occasionally they shared a prize—they won the West German Booksellers' and Publishers' Peace Prize—but, more frequently, each was honored separately. Swedish young people continued to feel Alva took an interest in issues they felt strongly about, and she received the Youth Peace Prize from a Swedish youth group.

Then, in 1980, Alva became the first person to receive the Albert Einstein Peace Prize. When this award was announced, particular mention was made of her writings. A spokesperson for the Einstein Foundation said they "had made an indelible [lasting] impression on the thought of the twentieth century." She also won an award from the United Nations Food and Agricultural Organization. In accepting this Ceres Medal, Alva joined a list of famous women, such as Coretta Scott King of the United States, who previously had won this prize.

In the meantime, Gunnar won awards of his own. In 1974 he shared the Nobel Economics Prize with Friedrich A.

van Hayek, an Austrian. When, by 1981, Alva's name had not appeared on the list of Nobel winners, Norwegian organizations raised funds to give her a special People's Peace Prize. They were trying to send a message to the Nobel selection committee. The same year Alva and other writers completed *Dynamics of European Nuclear Disarmament*, a study of vital decisions facing nations during the last decades of this century.

At last, in 1982, when she was eighty years old, Alva learned she would share the Nobel Peace Prize with Alfonso García Robles of Mexico. Their contribution, the Nobel committee said, was their "patient and meticulous [careful] work to create a foundation for international negotiations on mutual disarmament."

Robles, a former Mexican foreign minister who served as his country's representative to the United Nations, is credited with bringing about a 1967 treaty that established a nuclear-free zone in Latin America. He also played a key role in the UN's 1978 disarmament session. Alva was particularly pleased to share the award with Robles. She said, "Sweden and Mexico are leaders among the nonaligned countries fighting for disarmament."

With Alva's award, she and Gunnar became the first husband and wife to win Nobel Prizes in different categories (economics and peace). Couples who have won in the same category include: Marie and Pierre Curie, who were awarded half of the Physics Prize in 1903; Marie's daughter Irène Joliot-Curie and her husband Frédéric Joliot-Curie, winners of the 1935 Chemistry Prize; and Gerty and Carl Cori, who received half of the Physiology or Medicine Prize in 1947.

Although Alva was not well, the Myrdals traveled to

Oslo, Norway, so that she could receive her Nobel Prize in person. The following day she delivered her Nobel lecture. The Nobel Institute's director escorted her to the rostrum, supporting her by one arm. Once she began her speech, however, the audience forgot her age and ill health because she spoke with the energy and fire of her younger days.

"The age in which we live can only be characterized as one of barbarism [savage behavior]. Our civilization is in the process not only of being militarized, but also being brutalized," she said passionately.

While she attacked the willingness of many nations to produce and stockpile nuclear weapons, she also spoke out about brutal actions on a more personal level. "The cult of violence has so far permeated [spread throughout] the relations between people that we are compelled to witness an increase in everyday violence, violence on the streets and in homes. These are the examples we set for our young people," she noted.

Alva went on to mention that, in his will, Alfred Nobel had taken measures to encourage "the holding and promotion of peace congresses [conferences]." She suggested that, in the future, people who organized such conferences could become candidates for Nobel Prizes.

Alva's career has had many parts. She has been a diplomat, politician, educator, and writer. Her work has promoted equality between generations, sexes, social classes, and nations. More women, she hopes, will follow her example and work at an international level for world peace. "If only reason could prevail," she has said, "the. . . arms race could be defeated, so that the people of all nations can be winners instead of losers."

4.

Maria Goeppert Mayer

Physics Prize 1963

The blazing lights, set up for television cameras, made it impossible for Maria Goeppert Mayer to see the audience from where she sat on the stage. What was her husband, Joe, thinking, she wondered, as she tried to peer past the lights to locate him in the darkened auditorium. Soon she would cross the stage and receive the Nobel Physics Prize from the king of Sweden. Maria hoped she would not make any mistakes with so many people watching. A stroke three years before had almost completely paralyzed her left hand and arm, and even her right hand had little strength.

All went well. First Eugene Wigner, who had won half the Physics Prize, and then Maria Mayer and Hans Jensen, who had shared the other half, received their medals. After accepting hers, Maria backed away from the king. Keeping her face toward him in the traditional gesture of respect, she took her seat again. Relieved, she sat back to listen to the speeches for the other Nobel winners. She could not tell, but out in the audience Joe was sitting with tears in his eyes.

A German Childhood

Joe and Maria had been married for thirty-three years by the time this Nobel ceremony took place. They had met in Göttingen, a small city in Germany where Maria had been living since she was four. Her father, Friedrich, was a professor of pediatrics—the branch of medicine that deals with the care of children—and he also was the founder of a children's clinic. "He was the kind of person whom everybody loved," Maria later remembered.

Friedrich was very patient with Maria. Since she had no brothers or sisters, she went to him when she wanted a question answered. The two of them often walked into the hills surrounding Göttingen. Sometimes on these walks they would look for fossils or Friedrich would tell Maria the names of the trees and plants they saw.

The city where the Goeppert family lived was famous for its university, the Georgia Augusta University, known simply as Göttingen. Scholars came from many countries to study there. The city had stood almost unchanged for centuries and, during Maria's childhood, it still was surrounded by ancient walls. When visitors went to see the famous old church, they passed garden after garden, for practically every house had its own. Since a special kind of sausage was one of the town's specialties, delicious smells floated down the streets.

Maria's mother, who had taught French and piano before her marriage, enjoyed being the wife of a well-known professor. She liked to give parties where guests, flowers, and music overflowed their large house.

Especially good at mathematics and languages, Maria had no trouble learning at her elementary school. Outside of the classroom she was curious about many things and liked to explore the city with her friends. She stayed adventurous in spite of frequent headaches—ones she later called "terrible"—that often bothered her. The headaches and other childhood illnesses did not make as much of a difference as they might have because nothing could affect Maria's high spirits for long. The days at home, however, made her realize that, while it was fun to be around people, she could be alone and still find interesting things to do.

Not every girl has a world-changing murder to mark one of her birthdays, but Maria did. On June 28, 1914, the day Maria became eight years old, Archduke Ferdinand of Austria was assassinated. Just as one match can set fire to a pile of sticks ready to burn, his death was the spark that started World War I.

The carefree life of Göttingen stopped. Uniformed men marched off to battle, and wartime measures were put into effect by the German government. As the war went on, food became scarce and many families, including Maria's, were hungry most of the time. Because turnips were still available, everyone soon became very tired of eating turnip soup. Patients coming to see her father no longer had money. Instead, they brought what little food they could gather together to pay for the health care he provided.

By the time the war ended, Maria was a teenager. Gradually, as conditions in Germany improved, the big house was once again filled with guests. Maria's parents gave dances for her and her friends, and their home became a place where young people could have a good time. Sometimes these parties lasted past midnight because Maria's mother played the piano after the musicians hired for the evening had left.

To the University

When she was fifteen, Maria left public school to attend the Frauenstudium, a school where a small number of girls studied to enter the university. "It somehow was never discussed, but taken for granted by my parents as well as by me that I would go to the university. Yet, at that time, it was not. . .easy for a woman to do so," Maria commented. She was supposed to stay at this new school for three years, but after she had been there only two the school ran into financial problems and had to close.

Against the advice of her teachers, who thought she was too young and did not know enough, Maria decided that she would try to pass the university entrance examination. Since she had less than the normal number of years of preparation, this attempt was considered foolish. Maria and the other students were worried as they sat down to take the examination. After all, they would take one part of the exam every day for a week! Maria was successful, however, and became a university student.

Slim, small, and attractive, Maria was invited on many bicycle tours, mountain hikes, and skiing trips, favorite student pastimes. At the university she concentrated on mathematics and intended to become a teacher. In choosing this course of study, she was following both a tradition of her city and her family. For six generations on her father's side there had always been a university professor.

Göttingen had many leaders in the mathematics and physics fields, and each famous name attracted others to the university. For instance, David Hilbert, a mathematician, invited Max Born, a former student of his, to Göttingen. Born, a physicist, brought two more physicists, Enrico Fermi and James Franck. These men were among those beginning to make contributions that would be recognized as the most important scientific advances of their time. What was more, they would play a part in the development of Maria's career.

Physics is the science that deals with matter (anything that has weight and takes up space) and energy and how they interact. Some of the things physicists study include motion, light, heat, sound, and electricity. They also investigate atoms—the basic units that make up everything we know.

When Maria became a student at Göttingen in 1924, the physicists there were taking exciting steps toward understanding what was going on inside atoms. In their work they were helped by earlier discoveries. Ernest Rutherford already had shown that an atom has a central core—the nucleus—and particles called electrons that surround it. He also had found that the nucleus was positively charged and the electrons negatively charged.

Soon after Rutherford's discovery that the atom resembled a miniature solar system, with the electrons orbiting the nucleus as the planets orbit the sun, Niels Bohr proposed a new idea. He suggested that theories developed by other scientists, including Albert Einstein and Max Planck, could also be used to explain the behavior of the electrons in atoms. In brief, Bohr's quantum theory recognized that the electrons of an atom can have only certain energy levels. When an electron changes from one level to another, a quantum of light, or photon, having an energy equal to the difference of energy between the levels, either is given off or absorbed.

Scientists, eager to explore more of the atom's secrets, came together to discuss their thoughts and work. Göttingen was one of the places they met. They gradually realized new rules would have to be made to explain the workings of the atom.

While the physics field was changing rapidly, Maria was studying mathematics. Her closest friends were young men. Since she seemed shy and did not like to show the way she felt, it was easier to talk with male students about their work than to make conversation with young women she knew. Sometimes the men flirted with her, but Maria did not mind that at all.

One day at the university, Maria met the physicist Max Born. He invited her to attend the class he was on his way to teach, and she accepted. After class thirty or more students accompanied Born on a long walk, talking about physics as they rambled through the hills. Maria went along. She became fascinated by the discussion and soon made up her mind to concentrate her studies on physics instead of mathematics. "Mathematics began to seem too much like puzzle solving. Physics is puzzle solving too, but of puzzles created by nature, not by the mind of man," she observed. Maria would pursue her strong interest in physics despite a sad event in her family.

In 1927 Maria's father died unexpectedly. She and her mother were plunged into deep sorrow. He had told Maria many times that when she grew up he hoped she would have a career and keep stretching her mind. Maria was determined to honor her father's wish. She would make sure she completed her doctorate degree at the university.

During the next few years she worked at physics with some of the best physicists in the world. To some extent, Max Born took the place of Maria's father, guiding and teaching her.

94

An American Husband

Then, in 1929, someone new entered her life. His name was Joseph Mayer, and he was an American who had come to Göttingen to study. Mayer, a chemist, had received his Ph.D. degree from the University of California at Berkeley. Before leaving California, he had been told by friends that he should try to find a room to rent in a private home once he arrived in Germany. Many Göttingen families took in students as paying guests, and Maria's mother had done this since her husband's death.

The afternoon after coming to the town, Joe Mayer rang the doorbell of Maria's house. Because her mother was ill that day, Maria talked to Joe and showed him the room for rent. If he came back the next day, she said, she would have found out from her mother if he could rent it. Joe thought the blond young woman was very pretty. But he was annoyed because instead of answering his questions in German—a language he thought he had at least some skill in speaking— she insisted on replying in English. Maria had spent one school term in Cambridge, England, where she had practiced her English until she could speak and read it well.

Tall, lanky Joe did rent the room. Soon he found himself taking Maria places in the car he was able to buy with money from the American foundation that had sent him to Germany. A car was an unheard of luxury for Göttingen students. Some of the other men who had been dating Maria were jealous when Joe drove her away for an afternoon's swimming. He was a good swimmer, and the public pool let him show off his athletic talents.

Maria found Joe to be quick-thinking, humorous, and fun to be with. She also noticed their differences. He loved to argue about almost any subject, and sometimes he would lose his temper. Maria, on the other hand, always kept her emotions under control. Still, they soon knew they were in love and, in January 1930, they were married at the city hall. A party followed and then a honeymoon in another German city. When the Mayers returned, they stayed in the Goeppert house while Maria's mother visited relatives.

Maria was working long hours on her dissertation, a long research paper which she had to finish before she could receive her doctorate degree. She also had to get ready to take an examination. This test was a terrifying experience for most German students, since it was the only one they took from the time they entered the university until they received their Ph.D. All their years of work led up to this one chance for success or failure.

Maria finished her dissertation and went to take the final examination. A crowd of friends waited outside the building while she answered the questions. A cheer went up when they heard she had passed, and Joe took everyone out to celebrate.

The newly married couple was completely wrapped up in themselves and their work, for Joe—besides pursuing Maria—had his own studies. They did not notice that events in Germany were moving in a frightening direction. Widespread economic problems had brought on the Great Depression. People all over the world lost their jobs, and many families were close to starvation.

In this time of unrest, a political group called the National Socialist German Workers' Party began to gain power in Germany. This group became known as the Nazis. As part of their plan to grasp power, the Nazis became strongly anti-Jewish. Eventually they would force German

Jews to leave their homeland. Those who remained behind were hunted down and either killed outright or shipped to concentration camps. Many of the Göttingen physicists were Jewish and would flee to America for this reason.

In the spring of 1930, however, Maria and Joe never gave a thought to the troubling events in Germany. The university world of Göttingen was isolated from political upheaval.

A New Home Across the Ocean

Soon after Maria got her degree, she and Joe sailed to New York. Joe had accepted a position in the chemistry department of Johns Hopkins University in Baltimore, Maryland. Maria had become close to her mother, especially since her father's death, and she was homesick as they crossed the Atlantic. Once in America, there were many new things to get used to.

On her first day in Baltimore, Joe had to attend to some business. He suggested to Maria that she take a streetcar into the downtown part of the city to see the sights. Maria found the right streetcar and got on. When a conductor came to collect her fare, Maria asked him, in her almost perfect English, how much to pay. "A dime," he answered. Now although Maria knew the language, she had no idea which coin in her purse was a dime. She decided to bluff her way through the situation. The only trouble was, the coin she selected was a nickel. When she handed it to the conductor, he looked at her with a strange expression. After more rummaging in her purse, the woman sitting next to Maria finally helped her by showing her what a dime looked like.

Besides a new marriage and country, Maria had her

career to think about. At Johns Hopkins as at most other coeducational colleges in America, nepotism rules were in effect. These rules said that a college could not hire both a husband and wife. Although a wife was just as intelligent as her husband, and even if they both had doctorate degrees, the wife could not be given a regular professional position in the same college. Maria was a victim of these rules not only in Baltimore but also in later moves she and Joe made. The poor state of the American economy when she arrived in Baltimore did not help matters.

Johns Hopkins did say she could have an assistantship, which let her become involved in the scientific activities of the university. She also helped a faculty member who needed to write to colleagues in Germany. Any other work she did was to be done on a voluntary basis—without pay. The university also gave her a little room to use an an office. It was in what was called the attic of the science building. Since Maria was not one to complain or raise a fuss, she accepted these arrangements.

She and Joe lived in a rooming house for a few months because there was no point in finding a home of their own yet. They were going to a special summer physics session in Ann Arbor, Michigan. Enrico Fermi was one of the teachers at this session. He had been at Göttingen with the Mayers and was to give Maria important help in her later Nobel-winning work.

Back at Johns Hopkins that fall, Maria missed her mother and Germany a little less. The Mayers now had found a house, and she became friends with the wife of another member of the chemistry department.

No one at Johns Hopkins appreciated how much Maria knew about physics. This was partly because, in Göttingen, she had been involved in a special area within the physics field called quantum mechanics. Quantum mechanics grew out of the earlier developed quantum theory. At first it was accepted more by physicists in Europe than by those in America.

During her years in Baltimore, Maria was far from idle. She learned a great deal from a professor named Karl Herzfeld, who was working in an area of science that combined physics and chemistry. Both from working with him and from discussions with Joe, Maria broadened and deepened her knowledge. Throughout the early 1930s she wrote articles with both Herzfeld and Joe that, upon publication, first brought her name to the attention of American scientists.

Raising an American Family

Each summer the Mayers returned to Germany. Although Maria was glad to be with her mother, she realized she was unconsciously getting used to life in America. Also, Maria came to see what many other people already understood—the political pressure in her homeland was building like a volcano about to erupt.

When she learned she was to have a baby, she decided to become an American citizen. Maria wanted her child to have two American parents. The Mayers' daughter, Marianne, was born in 1933 at the same time the true ugliness of the Nazi hatred of Jews made itself known.

During the 1930s thousands of German Jews left their country whatever way they could. Many came to America. Those who were scientists brought with them new thoughts and information that acted like an injection of knowledge into the American scientific community. For Maria, their arrival—particularly that of the physicists—was an important event. In the coming years she would work with and be influenced by those who fled to safety.

Many of the new arrivals needed money for food, shelter, and clothing. For a time, Maria and Karl Herzfeld acted as treasurers for a group dedicated to aiding their German colleagues. The Mayers also opened their home to any refugee who needed a place to stay. One woman doctor whom they met on a summer trip to Germany lived with them for two years.

Maria was thrilled by her new baby. During her daughter's first year, she cut down on the number of hours she spent at Johns Hopkins so she could spend more time at home. After that, encouraged by Joe, she began to work again in earnest. Eventually, she was given the opportunity to present some lecture courses. And, for the first time, she was assigned graduate students of her own.

The Mayers kept time in their life for relaxation, however. They were well liked by faculty members and students. Maria's first graduate student, Robert Sachs, had the use of his father's forty-foot sailboat and sometimes invited the Mayers to go out with him on the Patapsco River near Baltimore.

In 1938 Maria learned her second child was on the way. While she was pregnant Joe lost his job, and the Mayers had to think about moving to a new home.

This setback was only temporary, though. Almost at once Joe had offers of two new positions, and he accepted one at Columbia University in New York City. Soon the Mayers joyfully announced the birth of their second child, a son they named Peter.

Just before leaving Johns Hopkins, they traveled to an important scientific conference in Washington, D.C. At this gathering of physicists, many of whom had come to America from Nazi Germany, they heard of a breakthrough that would influence Maria's career. This discovery was that the nucleus of the uranium atom could be split, releasing large amounts of energy. Already a few people realized that splitting such an atom meant an atomic weapon might be possible.

With Marianne and Peter the Mayers moved to the New York City area. Enrico Fermi, his wife Laura, and their children, as well as other people Maria and Joe knew, were living in Leonia, New Jersey. The Mayers decided to buy a house there. Leonia was not too far from their work in Manhattan, but was a better place than the city, they thought, to raise children.

The Mayers and the Fermis had met before, but now they became close friends. Laura was Jewish, and the Fermis had fled to America because of the anti-Jewish laws that had spread to other countries from Germany. Just a few months before, Enrico had won the Nobel Physics Prize for his experiments with radioactivity.

Scientists in Wartime

In September 1939, France and England declared war on Germany. On December 7, 1941, Japanese planes bombed Pearl Harbor, and the United States entered World War II. Both the day before Pearl Harbor and the day after, important events took place for Maria. On December 6 the American government decided to try to build an atomic weapon. Maria was soon to be involved in this effort along with many of the Mayers' friends and coworkers. And, on December 8, Maria was offered a half-time teaching job at an all-woman's school, Sarah Lawrence College in Bronxville,

New York. It was the first time since she had been in the United States that she had been given a position on her own merits, not just because she was the wife of an admired chemist.

The Mayers now began an extremely busy time of their lives. Maria taught mathematics, physics, and chemistry. She also drew up and taught a new course called Fundamental Physical Science. This course was described in the college catalog as presenting "man's knowledge of the universe and the atoms which compose it." In Maria's mind the various scientific fields were related to one another. The physical science course reflected her viewpoint by stressing the unity, not the differences, between the sciences.

When Maria started teaching at Sarah Lawrence, Joe began traveling to the Aberdeen Proving Ground in Maryland where he worked on weapons systems. He stayed in Maryland five days a week, worked at Columbia University a sixth day, and spent the seventh home with Maria and the children. The children and Maria did not like this arrangement because they hardly ever saw him.

Then, in a few months, Maria was offered a second job. Harold Urey, a friend and chemist at Columbia, asked her to join a secret research project at the university. This group was part of the widespread bomb development research known as the Manhattan Project. Members of the group were not allowed to discuss their work with anyone, not even their husbands and wives. For this reason Maria could not tell Joe what she was doing, although he did know she was at Columbia. Since having two jobs would keep her away from home every weekday, she hired a nursemaid to care for Marianne and Peter.

The Columbia project Maria joined eventually became

known as SAM, which stood for Substitute Alloy Materials. This was a coverup name that was used to avoid arousing anyone's interest. In fact, SAM members were working on a challenging effort.

Since Maria's student days, scientists had come to understand more and more atomic mysteries. In 1932 the picture of the atom's nucleus had changed with the discovery of the neutron. Researchers discovered that the nucleus has positively charged particles called protons and uncharged particles called neutrons. Surrounding the nucleus are the negatively charged electrons.

A chemical element is a substance in which all atoms are of the same kind. But, although atoms of a particular element have the same number of protons, they can have different numbers of neutrons. Each of these different atoms is known as an isotope. The SAM project was trying to separate the isotope uranium-235 from the much more abundant uranium-238. Uranium-235 was fissionable, or capable of having the nuclei of its atoms split. Uranium-238 was not fissionable. Because uranium-235 was fissionable, it could be used in making the atomic bomb.

The horrors of World War II are an ugly page of world history. And yet, the war made it possible for many American women, for the first time in their lives, to have equal job opportunities with men. On the SAM project Maria finally received the pay and recognition she deserved. "I was suddenly taken seriously, considered a good scientist," she said of those years. Although she was not usually assigned to the main focus of the SAM research, she was successful in the work she was given and eventually became the supervisor of twenty other scientists.

Maria flourished under the responsibilities of her job,

but she worried about its outcome. If America developed an atomic bomb, would it be dropped on Germany, the country where she had been born? For, although she was angered by the actions of the Nazis and their leader Hitler as much as anyone, she still loved her homeland where friends and relatives lived.

During this busy time Maria kept some hours for her children each day. They remember her reading out loud to them at night. After a while the strain of such long hours of hard work began to show. Maria found she had several health problems that had to be attended to. At one point pneumonia kept her in a hospital for several months.

The war was fought on both sides of the globe, and was still going on in the Pacific when it came to an end in Europe early in 1945. Joe was in the Pacific, having been sent there as part of his job. The atomic bomb was almost ready. Maria went to Los Alamos, New Mexico, where the bomb was being designed and built. She worked there with Edward Teller, an atomic physicist she had known for a number of years.

The first test of the bomb took place at Alamogordo, New Mexico, on July 16, 1945. Maria could have been there, but she wanted to rejoin Joe who had returned from the Pacific. Back in Leonia with their children, they decided to go on their first vacation since the beginning of the war. On August 6, while walking on the beach with Marianne and Peter, they were told by a neighbor of the dropping of the bomb on Hiroshima, Japan. This event released Maria from her pledge of secrecy, and she finally told Joe the details of her SAM work. A second more powerful bomb was dropped on another Japanese city, Nagasaki, three days later. Japan surrendered and the war was over.

A New Career in Chicago

Having taken a year's leave of absence from her teaching job at Sarah Lawrence during the war, Maria returned to the college when her SAM work ended. Columbia University had never recognized her work by giving her a teaching position. When an offer came from the University of Chicago, the new career opportunity was welcome.

The Mayers moved to Chicago where the Institute for Nuclear Studies was being established at the university. To the institute came many of the great men of physics, all glad to return to their careers and teaching after wartime. Edward Teller, Harold Urey, and Enrico Fermi were among those who went to Chicago at the same time as the Mayers. James Franck, Maria's old friend, already had a position there. It was unusual for so many strong scientific minds to be gathered in one location. And Maria was to be in the middle of this exciting learning environment.

After renting a house for a short time, Maria, Joe, and the children moved into a large home they found and bought. Maria loved the six fireplaces and high-ceilinged rooms. What was more, there was plenty of space on their property for gardens. Ever since her childhood she had enjoyed growing vegetables and flowers.

Joe was a full professor in chemistry, and Maria became an associate professor of physics as well as a member of the Institute for Nuclear Studies. She did not, however, receive a salary. The nepotism rules—still in effect—prevented the hiring of a husband and wife, even if they worked in different departments.

Since the Institute for Nuclear Studies did not yet have a building of its own, members carried on their work in their regular offices on campus. To help them know what other

105

members were doing, a weekly seminar was held. Joe became the leader of those informal meetings where anyone could talk about ongoing work. Maria came, too, struggling to understand the complicated ideas that flew back and forth across the room. She had decided to work as a nuclear physicist. But so far her background had not enabled her to learn much about the nucleus of the atom.

Maria was helped in her determination to grasp nuclear theory by her association with the Argonne National Laboratory, set up soon after the Mayers came to Chicago. Work at Argonne was directed toward finding peaceful uses of nuclear energy. It was there that the world's first controlled, self-sustaining chain reaction had taken place in 1942. In this process, through fission of atomic nuclei in a nuclear reactor, neutrons are produced. These neutrons then split other nuclei, releasing still more neutrons. Once begun, this process continues without any new actions being taken or any new substances being added.

Robert Sachs, the director of Argonne's theoretical physics division, was the same former graduate student who had taken the Mayers sailing during their Johns Hopkins days. Sachs knew of Maria's excellent work and respected the quality of her mind. When he was assembling the group of theoretical physicists who would work at the Argonne laboratory, he asked Maria if he could hire her—with a salary—as a senior physicist. "But I don't know anything about nuclear physics!" she observed. "Maria," Sachs replied, "you'll learn."

The Mayers were now happily settled in Chicago. Peter was nine and Marianne fourteen. Maria taught classes, served on committees, and directed graduate students in addition to carrying on her work at the Argonne. She relaxed by growing things in her gardens and on a glassed-in porch where she found orchids did well. Since both Joe and Maria liked to be around people, they gave parties often. In the warmer months friends came over for backyard barbecues.

A Special Project

About a year after coming to Chicago, Edward Teller asked Maria to work with him on a special project. It had to do with the origin of the chemical elements. When Maria agreed, she started a series of investigations that would take her to the discovery of her lifetime.

Maria and Teller realized some elements were much more abundant than could be explained by existing theories. Elements that were so abundant had to have a very stable nucleus, or one that did not break down or decay through radioactivity. Lead, for instance, has an extremely stable nucleus.

Why, Maria and Teller wondered, were the nuclei of these abundant elements so stable? Then Teller left town on business. While he was gone, Maria decided to look carefully at all the available information having to do with this problem. What she found was that these same nuclei contained certain even numbers of either neutrons or protons. As she later explained in her Nobel lecture, the first numbers that Maria found were 82 and 50. This meant that the abundant and stable nuclei she was studying had either 82 or 50 neutrons or 82 or 50 protons. Since this happened consistently, she believed it could not be accidental. The numbers must be a clue to the structure of the nuclei, Maria reasoned.

When she told other physicists about this interesting

fact—Teller was still away—a researcher at Argonne suggested that she read papers by W. M. Elsasser, a scientist she had known in Göttingen. Elsasser also had noticed that certain numbers kept occurring in connection with the stable nuclei. Later, though, he had abandoned his work on the subject.

When Teller returned, Maria told him about the special numbers 82 and 50—figures she and others had started to call "magic numbers." Teller was busy with other projects, however. Maria continued the research alone, although she often talked with Enrico Fermi about the problem she was wrestling with. She added more magic numbers so that there were now seven: 2, 8, 20, 28, 50, 82, 126. As long as the number of either protons or neutrons in an element's nucleus added up to one of the magic numbers, that nucleus was extremely stable.

Maria could think of little else. These numbers fascinated and tormented her. When she came home at night, she and Joe talked about them. Joe encouraged her to continue; he, too, had the feeling the numbers were important.

As she worked, Maria began to think that protons and neutrons might be thought of as arranging themselves in thin layers of shells, or three-dimensional groupings. The shells, she thought, fit inside one another like a series of containers, each one capable of holding a few more particles than the last. A theory similar to this had for years been very successful in describing the way electrons combine to form shells around an atom's nucleus. (Today's scientists prefer to describe electrons as moving in what they call "clouds.")

Maria became convinced that this shell-like construction, or model, could provide the answer to the puzzle of her magic numbers. In 1948 she put her ideas in a scientific paper that was published in a scholarly journal. But Maria realized there still was something missing.

One day Fermi and Maria were talking together about the shell model. Someone came to tell Fermi he was wanted on the telephone. "What about spin-orbit coupling?" he asked just before he walked out the door. Maria said, "Yes, that's the solution." "How can you know?" he replied and left the room. By the time he returned from his conversation, Maria had worked out the basic parts of a mathematical explanation. In just a few minutes she had done the work that would win her the Nobel Physics Prize.

Applying the idea of spin-orbit coupling to the shell model theory finally gave Maria the answer she needed. She once explained spin-orbit coupling to her daughter, Marianne, as being like a roomful of waltzing couples. Imagine the dancing couples spinning around while, at the same time, they orbit, or circle, a ballroom. Some couples could spin in one direction while others could spin in the opposite direction.

The dancers in Maria's example are really the protons and neutrons within an atom's nucleus. Like dancers, these particles can both spin and orbit, some in one direction and some in the other. In addition, there is a difference in energy between those that move clockwise and those that move counter-clockwise. Maria realized that this difference made it possible for the particles to be arranged in more orbits than had been thought possible before. And now her shell model made sense. Some arrangements of protons and neutrons are much more tightly bound in place than others. When this binding is at its tightest, a nucleus is very stable, and the magic numbers occur.

Maria was the first physicist to be able to explain clearly how the particles in the nucleus are arranged. It was now possible to think of the nucleus as an onion, with shells of particles building up in layers. Although she was sure her theory was correct, only later did scientists prove that spin-orbit coupling within nuclei does exist.

In spite of the importance of her discovery, Maria did not take credit for it immediately. Joe and her fellow physicists in Chicago worried that someone else would arrive at the same answer. Finally, in April 1950, *Physical Review* carried her article based on those few minutes when a flash of insight had come to her.

As it turned out, it was fortunate Maria did not wait any longer. A well-known German physicist, Hans Jensen, also had sent an article describing a shell model based on spin-orbit coupling to the same journal. The two could have become competitors, but Maria was generous as well as a professional and so was Jensen. When they met the following summer in Germany, they became enthusiastic about writing a book together.

The writing went slowly because Maria worked in a careful, orderly way while Jensen preferred to do things at the last minute. In 1955 their book, *Elementary Theory of Nuclear Shell Structure*, was published. It firmly connected their names with their shared discovery.

A New Job and the Prize

In 1959 Maria at long last received the offer of a full professorship in physics with a salary. The job was at the University of California on its San Diego campus. Joe was offered a professorship in chemistry. Before leaving Chicago they had one last large party, for the wedding of their daughter, Marianne. She married the son of a physicist the Mayers had known for years.

Getting settled in a new house by the Pacific took a lot of energy. Only a few weeks after arriving, Maria suffered the stroke that was to leave her partially paralyzed. Her recovery was slow, although she still taught and continued researching.

One morning four years later, a phone call from Stockholm notified Maria she had won the 1963 Nobel Physics Prize. She and Hans Jensen shared half the prize. The other half was awarded to Eugene Wigner, who also had done breakthrough work on the atom.

"Is it really true?" she said at first. And then, a few moments later, "Oh, how wonderful! I've always wanted to meet a king!" Joe was just as delighted, and ran to put some champagne in the refrigerator. He had awards of his own to be proud of.

When reporters descended on their house, Joe became worried that all the commotion might tire Maria. On their way to Sweden where Maria would accept the prize, they stopped for a short rest in Denmark. Before leaving California, a friend helped her choose a green brocade dress to wear for the Nobel ceremony. In Germany, Hans Jensen also bought new clothes. They were so different from his usual casual outfits that friends teased him when he arrived in Stockholm.

Nobel week passed like a dream. Maria was now in her late fifties, and the main part of the research that earned her the highest award in her field was more than a decade in the past. Nevertheless, she said, "To my surprise, winning the prize wasn't half as exciting as doing the work itself." On stage at the ceremony in Stockholm, she became the only living woman with a Nobel Prize in science. What was more, only one woman, Marie Curie, had won the Physics Prize before her.

Back in California, Maria continued to teach, do research, and participate in the continuing development of the shell model. By the late 1960s the Mayers' son, Peter, became an assistant professor. And, when their daughter had a baby, Maria became a proud grandmother.

Health problems had been making their effects felt for some time, however. A number of years before she had lost the hearing in one ear. Now she developed heart trouble. In 1972 she died of heart failure in San Diego.

According to her friends, Maria was quiet, modest, thoughtful, and elegant. While these are pleasant words, they do not seem to describe someone who, in addition to receiving the Nobel Prize, also became a member of the National Academy of Sciences and received honorary university degrees.

Her fellow scientists—perhaps most of all her husband Joe—could best appreciate the enthusiasm she had for her work. By earning a place in the worldwide community of great minds investigating the atom, Maria distinguished herself in one of the most creative efforts of the twentieth century.

5.

Pearl
S. Buck

Literature Prize 1938

As the ship left the harbor, the little family group stood solemnly on deck. The parents, Caroline and Absalom Sydenstricker, knew that it would be many years before they returned to their homeland, America. Along with their twelve-year-old son, Edgar, and their daughter, Pearl, they were on their way to China. It was 1892, and Pearl was then only three months old. Cradled in her mother's arms she was a pretty baby—so pretty that it was easy to see why she had been given the name of a gem that has a soft glowing shine.

The journey begun that day was one Pearl would often repeat during the lifetime that lay ahead. China and America, on opposite sides of the earth, would attract her equally, the way two magnets tug at a nail that lies between them. She would live the first half of her life in the Eastern world, and the second half in the Western world. Wherever she was, she would experience the pull of both worlds in her mind and emotions.

Caroline and Absalom were traveling to China because they had been living and working in that country. They had returned to America only because Caroline had wanted Pearl to be born there. As Presbyterian missionaries, their job was to bring the Christian religion to the Chinese. The people of China, however, already had their own beliefs based on centuries-old teachings. Many of the Christian ideas seemed strange to them, and so did the foreigners who brought these ideas to their country. Nevertheless, missionaries kept arriving, believing that they had been chosen by God to work with the Chinese.

Absalom took his missionary tasks seriously. He often bent his tall, thin body in prayer, and for many hours each day he studied his books. On board ship, though, he had to do something he had never done before. Caroline became seasick and could no longer nurse the new baby. Since Pearl refused to drink from a bottle, her father fed her by spoon and cup while the ship rolled from side to side on its long trip across the ocean.

At Home in China

Once in China, however, Pearl's world settled down. Her mother, recovered from the voyage, returned to her usual cheerful self. She often smelled of the flowers she liked to plant and care for, and she laughed easily. Caroline was the center of Pearl's life, for Absalom frequently left home for months at a time to preach. The home he left was a small house nestled in the low hills that rose gently around the city of Chinkiang. Here, Pearl spent many of her young years.

While most missionary families lived in homes surrounded by high walls, the Sydenstrickers believed they should live among the Chinese. Pearl had Chinese neighbors and, as she grew beyond infancy, she became friends with the children and grown-ups of these families. She thought of herself as a Chinese child, not as an American. In fact, she learned to speak Chinese before she spoke English. It was only when someone made fun of her blue eyes or light hair, so different from the brown eyes and dark hair of her playmates, that she realized she was a foreigner.

Someone else had a special place in Pearl's early life. The name that Pearl called her was Wang Amah. She was an elderly Chinese woman who served as a nurse and watched over Pearl and Edgar. The sight of her patient, wrinkled face and blue-coated figure came to mean love and contentment. "Tell me some stories," Pearl would often beg. "You know more stories than any woman in the world!" And, without looking up from the stocking she was darning, Wang Amah would begin a magical Chinese tale filled with devils and fairies, fearful dragons, and brave men who had powerful daggers.

The nurse had been a faithful servant to the family even before Pearl was born. Caroline had given birth to three other children, all of whom had died in China when they were very small. Together with Caroline, Wang Amah had rejoiced in each birth and wept over each death.

Missionaries were expected to take a sabbatical, or leave of absence, from their customary work on a regular basis. It had been time for one of these sabbaticals when Caroline learned she was pregnant again. She had been overjoyed to be able to return to her West Virginia home in America. There, in the house where she had grown up and where her family still lived, she had been sure she could rest and give birth to a healthy baby.

Caroline's strategy worked. Pearl was sturdy and strong, but her middle name, "Comfort," would always be a reminder of how much her birth had meant.

As she became old enough to explore the hills where she lived, Pearl grew used to seeing things that other missionary children—those sheltered behind high walls—did not. If there were rippling ponds, gardened valleys, and bamboo groves, there also were many hungry and ill Chinese people. Mothers with sick babies frequently came to ask Caroline for help. And, if the tiled roofs of the city with the Yangtze River glimmering in the distance made a pleasant picture from the windows of their home, Pearl knew that on the streets Chinese laborers, the coolies, sweated and strained as they carried sugar and rice on their backs.

During these years, Caroline had given birth to a baby boy she named Clyde. But Pearl did not have a younger brother for long. Clyde died of diptheria when he was four, and Pearl, then six, barely survived the same disease. The arrival of a new baby sister, Grace, the following year was a source of joy for Pearl, who missed her younger brother.

Every morning Pearl got up early, for her father would not seat himself at the breakfast table until the entire family had assembled there. Morning prayers followed breakfast. Each child was expected to recite a verse from the Bible. Even years later Pearl could remember how the rough matting on the floor hurt her knees as she knelt for what seemed like hours, listening to her father pray.

Learning about Literature

Then Pearl would do the lessons her mother assigned, studying English grammar, American and world history, and arithmetic. She hurried through them as fast as possible so she could be free to go outside and get on with what she thought of as "the real stuff of life."

Besides playing with the children who lived nearby, Pearl had another way to meet Chinese people. Her parents were the only missionaries she knew who invited Chinese visitors to spend the night in their guest room and eat at their table. Pearl noticed that these guests were very curious about American ways and pleased to be inside her home.

When Pearl was eight, Mr. Kung began coming to teach her Chinese reading and writing several afternoons a week. He was a Chinese gentleman who wore long robes and arranged his hair in the traditional pigtail. In their talks together, Pearl learned about Chinese history and philosophy. Mr. Kung had great respect for books, and he passed on his feelings to Pearl. He also told her that, in China, only certain kinds of writing were considered literature. The official literature was that written by upper-class scholars in the classical Chinese language. These writings were supposed to instruct readers, not to entertain them.

Literature, according to Mr. Kung, certainly did *not* include what are known as novels, the fictionalized stories of everyday men and women, told in an attention-getting way. Later, Pearl was to discover that, in fact, such stories did exist in China and had been loved for centuries. Many had been told out loud before being written down. But, because it was thought that only the common people enjoyed these tales, and because they were written in the ordinary language spoken on the streets, novels were frowned on by people like Mr. Kung. No respected writer, he observed, would ever write a novel.

Many times in Pearl's life she had to learn to accept ideas that seemed to contradict, or go against, each other.

She did understand what Mr. Kung was saying. After her lessons with him were over for the day, though, she often curled up with exactly the kind of book he had just been criticizing—a novel.

Pearl found these novels on a high shelf where her mother had hidden them. For, although Caroline's religious feelings led her to believe that reading such books was an idle pastime, she was unable to resist an exciting story. And, over the years, Caroline had managed to collect a few of the novels that were well known to English-speaking people. When Pearl discovered and began reading these books, she found they could make her feel sad, happy, or angry. Sometimes, especially when she was reading a novel by an author named Charles Dickens, she even forgot where she was until her mother called her for dinner.

For Pearl, Chinese and American customs and ideas existed side by side. She simply "shut the door" between her two worlds when she needed to. Caroline and Absalom believed in celebrating all the American holidays, and Pearl's neighborhood friends made sure she observed the Chinese ones.

On Halloween, for instance, Caroline and Pearl worked together to carve a round squash bought in the local market. That night, people passing by were surprised to see a grinning jack o'lantern shining in the dark of the Chinese street. The Fourth of July, Thanksgiving, and, of course, Christmas, were special days. But Pearl also joined in the Chinese festivals, including Chinese New Year and the Feast of Lanterns. In the spring, kites of every imaginable shape and color soared over the hills. Some were so large they needed a dozen men or more to launch them into the sky.

At about the same time she began reading novels,

Pearl—with her mother's encouragement—began to write about her experiences and feelings. She sent some of the things she wrote to the Shanghai *Mercury*, an English-language newspaper published in China. The *Mercury* offered cash prizes each month for the best stories and articles submitted by children. Pearl won so often that, by the time she was ten, she had come to count on the regular income. Not only did she have some pocket money, but she had the fun of seeing something she wrote in print.

Torn Between Two Worlds

In 1900, when Pearl was eight, her two worlds split violently apart. For many years foreign countries had been increasing their power in China. England, Germany, France, Russia, and Japan all wanted to have a say in China's affairs. The United States also became interested. The leaders of industry in these countries understood that during the years of the new century China would leave behind many of her ancient ways and begin to become a modern nation. To the foreigners' way of thinking, China was an opportunity that would never happen again. Think of the products her enormous population could use! What was more, many Chinese wanted railroads, steel mills, shipyards, and coal mines. The foreigners made it clear they would be more than happy to supply these needs, but in return they made many demands. What they really wanted was to divide China among themselves.

To back up their demands, the foreign nations sent warships and soldiers to China. A woman known as the Empress Dowager ruled China at this time. Although she was personally strong, her government was weak. She was bitterly opposed to what the foreigners were doing to her

country, but her troops—fighting with simple weapons—
could not stop those who used guns and other advanced
tools of warfare.

The Empress Dowager decided to make a desperate
attempt to free China from the foreigners' power. She listened to a group of terrorists, the Boxers, who promised
they could defeat the outsiders and return China to her own
people. Most importantly for Pearl's family, the Empress
Dowager ordered all foreigners, including the missionaries,
to leave China forever. She told her governors and the
Boxers to kill any white people who remained.

It took a while for the impact of this order to reach the
Sydenstrickers. The first sign came when the stream of
visitors to their house began to grow smaller. Soon days
passed without a Chinese friend's face. While the neighbors'
affection for Pearl and her family had not changed, they
were afraid to show this affection openly for fear they would
be punished. For the first time Pearl realized she could
never be truly Chinese. Her white skin meant she was part
of the race marked as China's enemy. During the rest of her
life, Pearl never forgot her feelings of sorrow and injustice
during these days.

Soon it became clear the family would have to leave
their home. Pearl went from room to room, unable to
believe what was happening. She watched her mother bury
some of their valuables to keep them from being stolen.
When the signal—a red flag flown from the top of a
building—was given at noon one day, Caroline and her
children hurried to join other families boarding the steam-
ship that would take them to safety in Shanghai. In that city
the white community had enough weapons for defense. Absalom decided to stay behind. His unshakeable faith made

him strong, and in place of fear he knew only the love of God.

Eight months passed before Absalom rejoined his family in Shanghai. Even his determination could no longer advance the Christian cause in China. Several of the churches he established were destroyed by fire, and no one wanted to hear him preach.

The Boxers and the Empress Dowager were defeated by the powerful foreign nations. In fact, the treaty signed at the close of the fighting left China worse off than before. Foreigners now had almost unlimited rights within the country, and other burdens such as heavy taxes were put into effect. Before, most Chinese had been willing to accept missionaries like the Sydenstrickers. Now they actively disliked all whites. Since it was time for the Sydenstrickers to have another sabbatical year, Caroline and Absalom decided to take the family to America.

It was a time of wonder for Pearl. She was nine years old and returning to the country of her birth. The family traveled across the Pacific by ship and into San Francisco harbor. How clean the city seemed compared with those in China! And there were luxuries Pearl had never used before: a built-in bathtub, for instance, and water running from faucets. In China there had been a tub that had to be filled by using buckets. Elevators were unexpected miracles.

Discovering America

Soon the family was on a train speeding eastward across America. More new sights were seen every day. Pearl and her younger sister had ice cream for the first time. Then they reached West Virginia and Caroline's home where Pearl had been born.

The lovely big white house, the green lawn, and maple trees were just as Caroline had described them to Pearl. Pearl's grandfather greeted her, as did many aunts, uncles, and cousins. After some weeks Pearl and her family went to visit Edgar, Pearl's older brother. He was now a university student in Virginia. That August the family went back to the white house in West Virginia. It was a particularly happy time for Pearl, but it did not last long. After a winter in Lexington, Virginia, the Sydenstrickers returned to China. Pearl had to change worlds again.

A Different China

Now the years passed quickly. Although she was back in her China house, Pearl was not a child anymore. China was different, too. European nations now had so much power within China that they could do just about anything they wanted. While the Chinese feared the white people and seemed to have handed over control of their country to them, they deeply resented the foreigners. Pearl's Chinese teacher, Mr. Kung, warned her that he knew "the storm is still rising." He told her that one day she and her people would have to leave China forever.

But, in the meantime, many Chinese sought to gain positions of influence and power by pleasing the foreigners. One way to do this was to become a Christian. Absalom suddenly found Chinese were interested in joining his religion. He began to travel widely and opened many churches.

Caroline realized Pearl soon would need to go to America to attend college. Although Pearl had attended some schools for short times, she had not had any lasting contact with American girls her own age. Her Chinese girlfriends were already being readied for marriage. In the Chinese tradition, their feet were tightly bound so that they could not run and play. Tiny feet were thought of as beautiful, and any girl who wanted her parents to arrange an honorable marriage for her needed to stop her feet from growing large.

Caroline decided to send Pearl to boarding school in Shanghai for a year. This experience was not a success. Miss Jewell, one of two sisters who ran the school, seemed stern and severe. Pearl took no great interest in her classes since she was more advanced in many subjects than the other girls, thanks to her mother's daily lessons.

Miss Jewell believed young women should help people less fortunate than themselves. She took Pearl to a home for mistreated Chinese girls. There, Pearl taught needlework. But as the girls bent over their embroidery, they told her frightening tales of how they had been sold into slavery when their families could no longer feed them during times of famine. Miss Jewell also made sure Pearl attended prayer meetings. But these differed from those Absalom led. The religious group Miss Jewell belonged to talked a great deal about sinners and how they would burn forever in hell. Nightmares began to keep Pearl from sleeping.

When she returned home for a vacation and told her parents about Miss Jewell's school, they felt she should not return. Instead, they decided she was ready to go to college in America. This time, instead of crossing the Pacific Ocean, the family would travel the other way around the globe and spend a few months in Europe.

College in America

Traveling by boat and then by train, Absalom, Caroline, Pearl, and Grace made their way north to Manchuria and then across the long, desolate reaches of Russia. Finally they were in Europe. Pearl especially liked England, which she felt she already knew from descriptions in the novels she had read.

Then it was on to America. Pearl's family had selected Randolph-Macon in Virginia as the college she would attend. Caroline approved of this all-girls' school because, as she told Pearl, "the education there was planned to be exactly what a man would get." A few months after bringing Pearl to the college, Absalom, Caroline, and Grace returned to China. It was four years before Pearl saw them again.

Without meaning to, Pearl's classmates made her realize how different she was from them. "Girls came in groups to stare at me," she remembered later. In her Chinese-made clothes and braided hair, Pearl looked nothing like an American college student. However, she was determined to fit in. She bought some new dresses and changed her hairstyle. If American girls her age talked about boys and dancing, she would too.

Pearl was successful. At least outwardly she seemed to be like the other students, and she quickly made friends. Her experiences in China, however, made her act like an adult. Unlike the other students, from her travels she had gained a broad knowledge and interest in people who lived in other countries.

By the time she was a junior, she had become so popular that she was elected president of her class. In her senior year she competed for and won prizes for both the best short story and best poem. During most of her college vacations, Pearl stayed with her brother, Edgar, who was now married and living nearby. She helped care for his small daughter and infant son. She also tutored other college students to earn some money.

In 1914 Pearl graduated from college. Recalling how she felt at that time, she said, "My attempt, successful enough in its own way, to be like other American girls, was not permanent, I fear, and after my graduation I was faced with my two worlds again. Which should I choose? Should I stay to become permanently American, or should I go home again to China?"

Pearl decided to stay in America. She knew she loved her country, and she wanted to see more of it. To earn her living, she took a job as a teaching assistant at Randolph-Macon. The plans she made, however, changed when she received a letter from Absalom. He said that her mother was very ill with a disease called sprue. This disease can be treated now, but then no one knew a way to help Caroline. With Grace still a teenager and Absalom often away on missionary business, Caroline was more or less alone. Wang Amah, the family's old servant, had died a few years before. Pearl did not hesitate. She found someone to take over her job, packed her bags, and set out again by ship for China.

A Family in Need

When the ship came to Shanghai, only Absalom and Grace were there to meet Pearl. Caroline had not been strong enough to make the trip. But she was waiting at the train station when Pearl reached what she called her "home town" of Chinkiang. Even though Caroline was painfully thin and weak, her smile was the same. Friends and neighbors also had come along, so Pearl was welcomed back to China with a celebration. "Now that you're here," Caroline told Pearl, "I'm going to put up a strong fight against this illness."

Together, Pearl and Caroline tried everything. Different foods were supposed to help, and some seemed to for a while. Over the months that followed Caroline managed to gain enough strength to be moved to the family's summer house—a little stone cottage in the mountains. Here, in Kuling, white families had found the cool air and mountain streams kept them healthier than in the hot cities.

Since Kuling seemed to agree with Caroline, they stayed even when summer ended. For a year Pearl nursed her mother. She understood that the contrast between her isolated, sheltered life and what was happening in the world could not have been greater. In Europe, World War I was raging, but all she knew about it came from brief reports in English-language newspapers that reached Kuling once a week.

China, too, was undergoing changes Pearl had not had a chance to experience. The Empress Dowager had died in 1908, the last in a long line of rulers of the Manchu dynasty. What form of government would there be in China now? No one was sure. Many Chinese supported a leader named Sun Yat-sen who wanted to establish a constitutional form of government like that of the United States. There were other powerful figures with their own ideas, however, and China was going through troubled times.

Finally, Caroline was well enough to stay in Kuling in the care of friends and neighbors. Pearl returned to Chinkiang and kept house for her father while teaching at a missionary school for Chinese boys. While she enjoyed her teaching, she felt tied down by the strict religious practices surrounding her.

When she was invited out on dates by young men who were working in China for American companies, the missionary women disapproved. Pearl was restless and ready to change her life. Many of her Chinese friends had married men chosen by their parents; some had children. Then, seemingly in answer to her wishes, Pearl met a tall, handsome young American, John Lossing Buck. Pearl called him by his middle name.

A Troubled Marriage

Lossing was employed by the Presbyterian Missionary Board to teach agriculture to the Chinese. Pearl soon believed she loved him. Although he did not like books as she did and seemed to find it difficult to carry on the kind of interesting conversations Pearl always had had with her parents, Pearl felt he might change with time. After seeing her only a few times, Lossing proposed marriage. Her parents, seeing how different the two young people were, tried to discourage Pearl. But she had made up her mind. Pearl and Lossing were married in 1917 and soon settled far from Chinkiang in a town in the northern part of China.

Since Lossing's job was to go among the Chinese peasants discussing agricultural methods, Pearl frequently went with him. Many times she was the first white woman the Chinese in this area had ever seen. She talked with the women and children while Lossing talked with the men. The lives of the people she met were ruled by the seasons, because their families had been farmers for generations. These peasants, Pearl found, "were closest to the earth, to birth and death, to laughter and to weeping."

Her marriage, she realized quite soon, was not going to be all she had hoped. Although Lossing was a good man, he and Pearl had little in common. His imagination did not equal hers, and she longed for someone with whom she could share the ideas that crowded her mind.

But Pearl had been influenced by Chinese women. Since they never spoke of their dissatisfactions to their husbands, Pearl never mentioned her distress to Lossing. She worked to make their new home a cheerful, pleasant place, and busied herself painting walls and making curtains. As always, because she spoke fluent Chinese, she became friends with her neighbors and went to weddings and other family affairs.

An American doctor frequently called on Pearl to act as his nurse. She was able to explain to his patients what he was doing so they would not be frightened. Then Pearl became head of a school for young girls in the town. This job helped her forget that at home, instead of a companion, she had someone she later called, in an autobiography, "the man in the house."

After almost three years in northern China, Lossing accepted a job teaching at the University of Nanking. He and Pearl moved south. Life in the city of Nanking was completely different from that in the farming community they had just left. Modern ideas coming from Western countries were beginning to be accepted by many Chinese, especially the young university students. Ancient customs were being questioned, and political and social revolution were in the air. It was a fascinating time to be in China.

Joys and Sorrows

During the first year in Nanking, 1921, two events changed Pearl's life. She gave birth to a daughter, Carol, and, for a time, thought of nothing else but her joy in this new person. But Pearl's mother had never completely recovered from her illness, and now she died.

Filled with the need to keep her mother's memory alive,

Pearl began to write about her. She told herself that the word portrait she made was for Carol, who would never have the chance to know her grandmother. When the manuscript was finished, Pearl put it away in a safe place, intending to keep it until Carol was old enough to read it. Pearl had no idea that what she had written would later become a book that would help make her famous.

Pearl kept busy. She taught in more than one of the city's universities, and also expanded her household to include her father and sister Grace, who had returned from college in America. Grace stayed with Pearl until she married.

Having started to write in earnest, Pearl found it easy to continue. She used an attic room in her home that had a window with a view of her favorite mountain. She wrote a short article on China for an American magazine, the *Atlantic Monthly*. When the article was accepted, she realized that her lifelong love of reading and writing had prepared her for a career.

Writers are always told to write about what they know best and, for Pearl, this meant the Chinese people. To her amazement, she found that American readers were interested in her favorite subject. The editors of other magazines soon accepted articles.

Real life events, however, had a way of pushing aside Pearl's writing. In 1925 it was time for Lossing to take a year's leave of absence from his work. Pearl had been aware for some time that something was wrong with their daughter. Although Carol's body was healthy, she could not talk or walk well, and she had trouble following directions. The couple decided to spend a year in America and get expert medical advice. They also would study at Cornell University in Ithaca, New York, for graduate degrees.

On the ship to America, Pearl began to write again. This story, based on the conflict in China between old and new ideas, was a work of fiction. Pearl finished the story before the boat docked. Some months later, settled in Ithaca, she sent it to *Asia Magazine*. From the editor she received a letter of acceptance and a check. Then Pearl won a writing prize offered by Cornell. This time she received enough money to buy a warm winter coat, a necessity she had not been able to afford on the family's small income.

Good news, however, was balanced by bad—some of the worst, in fact, Pearl was ever to hear. At a famous medical clinic, Pearl learned that Carol would never be normal. She had a condition that meant her mind would remain that of a child of four, although her body would continue to grow. Doctors today can treat this condition and prevent brain damage. But, at the time Carol needed it, there was no such treatment. Physicians advised Pearl to place Carol in a home for the mentally retarded. But Pearl could not yet bring herself to do this.

In her unhappiness she decided to adopt a child, since, because of an earlier operation, she could no longer have a child by birth. Pearl found a baby she wanted in a small orphanage. With her usual feeling for the unfortunates of the world, the baby she chose was the smallest and weakest offered for adoption. Within a few weeks, the baby—named Janice—began to gain weight. Pearl realized this child would flourish. Janice was the first of many babies who would find their way into Pearl's heart and home.

Then the year was over. The Bucks each had earned a master's degree. With Carol and Janice they packed their belongings and went back to China.

The China they returned to was poised on the edge of revolution. A political group, the Nationalists, led by Chiang Kai-shek, was attempting to bring about a new kind of rule. Rumors began to reach Nanking, where the Bucks were living, that white people, seen as enemies of China, were being killed in the northern part of the country. Pearl's sister, Grace, arrived with her husband and baby. They were fleeing the revolutionary troops. In spite of warnings to leave, the Bucks and their relatives decided to stay. After all, they reasoned, they were in sympathy with many of the demands being made by the Nationalists.

When the armies entered the city, however, the looting and killing were worse than expected. Leaving their house so quickly that their breakfast remained uneaten on the table, they rushed off looking for a place to take refuge.

They were rescued by a Chinese woman whom Pearl had once helped. This woman hid the group of white people in a room of her tiny hut. There they waited in terror all day, hearing the sounds of destruction around them. Only when artillery fired by American warships echoed across the city did the revolutionary armies retreat. The white families were taken to safety by ship. When she stepped onto the dock at Shanghai, Pearl realized she and her family had lost everything they owned. Her books and the manuscripts she had been writing were, she believed, gone forever.

The Bucks went to Japan for a year until it was safe to return to China. Eventually they made their way back to Nanking. There, although the house had been looted, Pearl found one manuscript unharmed. It was the portrait of her mother she had written and put carefully away.

Not long afterward, Pearl at last decided to place Carol in a home for retarded people in America. In 1929 she took her daughter to the place she had selected, the Training School of Vineland, New Jersey. There Carol would live, protected and cared for lovingly. While she was staying with friends in America, Pearl received exciting news. Two stories she had written had been accepted by a publisher, the John Day Company. The stories would be combined in one book to be called *East Wind: West Wind.*

A Growing Writer

Richard Walsh, the chief editor of the publishing company, asked Pearl to come to New York City to make some changes in her manuscript. When they met she thought him handsome and polite. Richard found her fascinating. He realized that although she wrote of birth and death, famine and revolution, his new writer was innocent about worldly things.

Richard told Pearl he had agreed to publish *East Wind: West Wind* not because, as he frankly said, he thought "it was a very good book," but because it showed the author "might continue to grow." In fact, he had accepted the book only after Pearl's agent—the person she had hired to help her sell what she wrote—had submitted it to many other publishers. All of them had turned the book down.

Pearl remembered Richard's encouragement when she returned to China. By now, attitudes in China had changed. Novels were no longer scorned, but eagerly read and talked about. Pearl sat at her attic desk and began writing.

Pearl had a remarkable memory, and all the experiences of her life were stored away, waiting to be released. As she worked, people and events came easily to life on paper. She wrote of the ordinary lives of a Chinese peasant family, much like the ones she had met when she had lived with her husband in northern China. Yet, while the characters she created were individuals, they also represented millions of people all over the world—those who worked with their hands year after year without thought or hope of change. Pearl's writing style was simple and direct. She managed to tell a story that would keep readers turning one page after another while, at the same time, revealing the dignity and wisdom of a wife, a husband, and their family.

Pearl mailed the manuscript to Richard Walsh in New York. Richard soon wrote back, saying "I believe you have written a book of permanent importance, one that will rank with the great novels of the soil." The word *soil* was significant. The people in Pearl's book were farmers. Their survival was tied to their plots of land. For this reason, Richard chose to title the book *The Good Earth*.

The Good Earth had immediate success. It became one of the all-time best-sellers in the history of American fiction. The United States was in the midst of a frightening time known as the Great Depression. Millions of people lost their jobs. Many families did not have enough to eat. Those who read Pearl's book felt a closeness to the people she described, for they, too, were struggling to survive. But, since the customs and life of Chinese peasants seemed strange and different to Americans, the book also appealed to readers' sense of adventure. It gave them something to think about besides their own troubles.

In other countries *The Good Earth* also was enormously successful. Eventually it was translated into more than sixty languages. Over the years the book earned Pearl a great deal of money. Once it appeared, she was no longer a women writing alone in an attic room in China. She was an important author. The year after its publication, Pearl won the Pulitzer Prize, an award given for distinguished American writing.

Now at the peak of her writing career, Pearl wrote at an astonishing rate. Two novels, *Sons* and *A House Divided*, continued the story begun in *The Good Earth*. These works became a trilogy, a series of three books. In addition, she wrote *The Mother*, the story of a Chinese peasant woman. During these same years, Pearl also translated a classic Chinese novel into English. When published, it was given the title *All Men Are Brothers*.

Pearl's family continued to be a major subject of her writing. Her father died in 1931 at the age of eighty. During his last years, when he had lived with Pearl, they had grown much closer than they had been when Pearl was a child. Soon after he died, Pearl began to write his biography. This book, *Fighting Angel*, was published in 1936, the same year as *The Exile*, the story of Pearl's mother. *The Exile* was the manuscript that had survived the looting of Pearl's home in Nanking. These two biographies were given excellent reviews.

A Hard Personal Choice

While her writing was progressing in great leaps, her personal life was in confusion. Pearl's marriage did not give her happiness. In addition, she missed and worried about Carol, her daughter who was now in New Jersey. Richard Walsh was urging her to come to New York to enjoy the fame *The Good Earth* had brought her. Since Pearl's husband wanted to complete his Ph.D. degree at Cornell, the couple decided to return to the United States with Janice.

Once there, Pearl appeared at a magnificent banquet held in her honor at a famous New York City hotel. Leaders of New York's literary scene came. Many found it hard to believe the timid, shy woman they saw was the author of a book that had, by now, sold nearly two million copies. For Pearl, unaccustomed to being treated as a famous person, the attention was overwhelming. Richard Walsh was a source of guidance and support.

After the banquet Pearl lived at Cornell with her husband and Janice. She also had a chance to visit Carol, who was doing well in her new home. New York City, however, was where she felt most stimulated and alive. Richard introduced her to writers, artists, editors. Pearl began to enjoy a new way of life. She and Richard often had lunch together, and what had begun as a business relationship blossomed into love. Although Richard, too, was married, he felt both he and Pearl deserved a second chance to find a kind of contentment neither had had before.

Pearl, however, could not make up her mind. Should she leave her husband? The missionary beliefs and the Chinese respect for family life she had grown up with held her back.

Pearl managed to crowd an amazing number of events into her year in America. In many ways, her life seemed to be splitting into pieces. She was struggling to balance the demands of her new fame with the need to continue to write. She knew that soon she would have to make a final decision about which of her two worlds she was going to live in. And, on top of everything else, *The Good Earth* opened as a play in New York. Although Pearl had not written the stage version herself, it still was disappointing when the play did not get good reviews from the drama critics. Nevertheless, this taste of the stage was enough to make Pearl begin to write for the theater.

Fortunately, Pearl had no trouble concentrating on one part of her life, even though another part might be in upheaval. Next she became interested in changing what she believed to be a great flaw in American society. Because she had been isolated in China for so many years, she had never learned that in the United States black people were not given the same opportunities as whites. What was more, she found out that blacks often suffered from unspeakable acts of cruelty and injustice. Pearl was horrified. Having once been in fear for her own life in Nanking, she vividly remembered what it was like to be hated because of the color of her skin. She had found something to fight for. In speeches and meetings, she became a champion of equality for blacks.

After Lossing received his Ph.D., he and Pearl, along with Janice, returned to China. On the way, Pearl told him that she and Richard loved one another. Using income from her books and magazine articles, Pearl had already given gifts of money, not only to Lossing, but to his parents. She also had set up a fund to take care of Carol and to support research to help the mentally retarded. She and Lossing agreed she should have a time of freedom to clear her thoughts and make decisions for the future.

In the following few years, Pearl took her life apart and put it back together again in a new way. The old China she had grown up with and loved had changed. Pearl realized she could not continue to keep one foot in the East and the other in the West. Now in her forties, she decided to spend the second half of her life in America.

Ater saying "no" several times to Richard's proposal of marriage, Pearl finally settled her mind and said "yes." In 1935 they both obtained divorces and were married. In the meantime, Pearl had bought an old stone farmhouse in

Bucks County, Pennsylvania. Here Pearl and her new husband settled. This same year she received the William Dean Howells medal for *The Good Earth.*

A New Beginning

Because Pearl and Richard wanted children and Pearl could not give birth to any, they adopted four infants. First were two boys and, a year and a half later, another boy and a girl. Since the couple also had an apartment in New York City, they found themselves traveling with babies, diapers, and bottles between two homes. A housekeeper, nursemaid, and cook were hired. Pearl was full of joy. She had found a man whose mind and interests matched her own.

While concentrating on getting Pearl to marry him, Richard had given the day-to-day operation of his publishing firm to someone on his staff. Now he found the John Day Company was in danger of going out of business. By using all available sources, Richard was just barely able to save the firm. Since John Day was still desperate for cash, Pearl became a part-time editor there. People began to have confidence in the firm again when they learned she was giving her support.

Pearl also had several new family concerns. Not long before, her sister Grace had had a daughter. During the birth, however, there was damage to the baby's nerves, and doctors now told Grace the child would always be completely helpless. Grace and her husband did not have much money. Concerned about the welfare of her sister's baby, Pearl took on the responsibility of paying for her care. Pearl also bought a home near the Bucks County farmhouse for her brother, Edgar, who was not in good health.

In 1936 the success of both *The Exile* and *Fighting*

Angel relieved Pearl of some of her worries about money. She also received the honor of becoming a member of The National Institute of Arts and Letters.

The events of Pearl's life always became a part of the novels she wrote. Sometimes it was easy to see a certain character resembled someone she knew in real life. This was especially true of a manuscript Pearl now finished and handed to Richard.

This time the story was set in America, not China. When Richard read what Pearl had written, he decided it revealed too much. The heartbreak involved in having a retarded child was even part of the story. He decided not to publish it. With the title, *The Time Is Noon*, it was finally released, but not until long afterward. Pearl later admitted that her husband's action had hurt her deeply. Yet at the time she hid her feelings and started another novel, one that would be called *This Proud Heart*.

Although this book is about a sculptor, not a writer, Pearl put a lot of herself into the heroine, Susan Gaylord. Susan discovers no one man is able to fulfill all her needs. But she also learns that her love of her work is the one unchanging thing in her life.

On February 2, 1937, a movie based on *The Good Earth* opened and became an overnight sensation. The movie's leading actress, Luise Rainer, won an Oscar for her performance, the film industry's top award. Pearl saw the movie and delighted in its popularity.

She also continued to have an interest in writing a play that would be successful in New York. For a while in the late 1930s, it looked as if a famous actress would be willing to play in one of Pearl's plays, but the plans fell through. Over the years Pearl was to write more than twenty-five plays.

Few, though, would be produced, and not one would be a hit. It was an area where even her strong determination could not prevail.

Surprised by the Prize

By 1938, Pearl was no longer confident of her writing ability. The novels with Chinese themes that followed *The Good Earth* were not received as well as that best-seller. And *This Proud Heart*, her attempt to write about American life, had not been praised by the critics even though millions of women had read it.

Working at her desk one morning, Pearl was startled when her secretary burst into the room. "You've won the Nobel Prize!" she cried out. Pearl was completely taken by surprise. Winning the award had been the furthest thing from her mind. She was the first American woman ever to win the Nobel Prize in literature.

The Nobel Prize ceremony was a glorious occasion for Pearl. Although she knew some people resented the fact that a woman who had spent much of her life in China was receiving the prize as an American, she was pleased by the wording of the Nobel citation. It read, "For her rich and genuine epic descriptions of peasant life in China and for her biographical masterpieces." Pearl Buck had won this highest honor not only for *The Good Earth*, but also for her other work, including the biographies of her parents.

Richard and a daughter from his first marriage, came to Sweden with Pearl. In honor of the Swedish king, the winners were told they should walk backwards to retake their seats after receiving their prizes. Pearl won the audience's applause when she did this successfully in spite of her long, elaborate dress which threatened to trip her.

Dinner for a thousand guests followed, and Pearl was seated close to the king. Parties and press conferences, as well as a special winter festival, became memories to be treasured. But on the ship home, tired and happy, Pearl looked forward to returning to the Pennsylvania farmhouse and to seeing Janice and her other children.

In the Nobel Prize lecture she had just given in Sweden, she had spoken of the history of the Chinese novel. But all writers of novels—whatever their nationality—had something in common, she said. Novelists, herself included, traced their beginnings to village storytellers. It was a novelist's job to reach out and grab readers' interest by telling tales of ordinary people in fascinating ways.

Life as a Famous Author

Pearl received the Nobel Prize in 1938 when she was forty-six. She lived another thirty-four years. During that time she never stopped writing, but there are many who believe most of her best work was behind her. Some literature experts think that in her later writings she tried too much to teach and not entertain.

One thing is certain. She was now able to do what she wanted. Winning the top literature award freed her from worry over reviews of her books and from doubt about her writing skill. From then on, she wrote what she chose and what she believed her readers would enjoy.

From 1939 to 1949, ten more of Pearl's novels were published. She also continued to write magazine and newspaper articles and to give speeches. In addition to working for equal rights for blacks, she spoke out on other issues. Many of them had to do with her belief that women should play a more vigorous role in modern life.

Understanding that she was seen as an expert on Chinese themes, Pearl decided to try out a new and daring plan when she wanted to write about America. She used the pseudonym, or pen name, of John Sedges. That way, she thought, few people would realize she was the author, and the books would be better received.

The plan worked. *The Townsman* by John Sedges sold well. Four more books under this pen name appeared. Eventually everyone knew what a few had suspected—John Sedges was really Pearl Buck. But by that time she had proved her point. She could write about America successfully.

During these same years Pearl also kept on writing under her own name. *Pavilion of Women,* another novel set in China, was second only to *The Good Earth* in number of sales. Then, in 1949, Pearl decided to share the story of her retarded daughter. *The Child Who Never Grew* is about Carol, who still lived at the Training School in New Jersey. Millions of people all over the world cried when they read this book. But, at the same time, it gave courage to the parents of other retarded children who realized Pearl Buck had been touched by the same tragedy that haunted them.

Pearl never stopped hoping the two parts of the world she loved could come to a better understanding. In 1941 she started the East and West Association. Through this group, funded in a large part by Pearl's efforts, Asians came to the United States, and Americans went to China. In 1949, the Communists gained control of China, and Chiang Kai-shek had to flee to the island of Taiwan. Pearl, in articles and speeches, urged the United States to "keep channels open to the Chinese people." Few Americans listened.

During the late 1940s, Pearl found still another outlet

for her energy. Social service agencies had trouble finding homes for children whose parents were of different racial backgrounds. Many of these children were born to Asian women, having been fathered by American military men abroad. Treated as outcasts by their mothers' families, the children often were neglected or abandoned.

Pearl called on her friends for donations of their time and money. It did not take long before she had collected quite a few babies and hired a husband and wife to care for them. The home she started became known as Welcome House. After a magazine carried a story about the children, people began to adopt them. Over the years, through Welcome House and another organization she founded, the Pearl S. Buck Foundation, thousands of children—both in America and abroad—found families to love and care for them. Pearl also took more children into her own home.

During the 1950s she wrote her autobiography, *My Several Worlds*, as well as *Imperial Woman*, a novel about the Empress Dowager, ruler of China when Pearl had been young. In 1953 Richard suffered a stroke. After a seven-year period of declining health, he died in 1960. Pearl was in Japan when he died, having gone there to work on a film production of a children's book she had written. Because Richard had not been well for so long, Pearl had, in a sense, already said good-bye to the man she loved. As always, she found comfort by writing about her feelings. In *A Bridge for Passing* she wrote about her response to Richard's death.

An Extraordinary Life

In the course of her life Pearl had, besides her two husbands, several male friends who influenced her as a person and as a writer. In her later years she continued to attract men. After Richard's death, Ernest Hocking— then eighty-eight—found in Pearl an ideal companion. The two met in New England and wrote many letters in which they mentioned their affection for one another.

In the last decades of her life, Pearl was more well known than ever. At a dinner party for Nobel Prize winners given by President John F. Kennedy and his wife, she was the only prize-winning woman. In 1966, when she was seventy-four, a national poll showed she was among the ten most admired American women. As she traveled across the United States raising money for her various projects, her name remained in newspaper headlines. Above all, her books stayed on the best-seller lists year after year.

A few months before Pearl's eightieth birthday, Chinese government officials refused to allow her to make a last visit to China. They said they did not like things she had written about their country. Deeply disappointed, Pearl was cheered by her birthday celebration. In a large chair, she received friends and relatives like a queen. Not long after, she died and was buried, as she had wished, under a large tree on the grounds of her Pennsylvania farmhouse.

Pearl Buck had led an amazing life—a life she would have been the first to agree could be used as material for a fascinating play. Her many interests and personal conflicts might have discouraged her from using her writing talent. But Pearl, expecting the best from others, also demanded a great deal of herself. She never stopped struggling to transform her own experiences into stories that would reach readers' deepest feelings. From two worlds she made one art.

6.
Dorothy Crowfoot Hodgkin

Chemistry Prize 1964

If the impossible could have happened, it would have been snowing in Cairo, Egypt, when Dorothy Crowfoot was born there in 1910. Since people living in Cairo's warm climate never expect to see snow unless they travel to a colder place, it is just as well snowflakes were not drifting down to cover the earth. But, if nature had decided to play such a joke that day, it would have been an excellent forecast for the future. Dorothy was going to spend her life studying different kinds of crystals, and what we see when it snows are really tiny ice crystals.

Crystals surround us, although we usually are not aware of them. By taking a swim in the ocean, for instance, you collect crystals without even trying. If you come out of the ocean, sit in the sun until you are dry, and then lick the back of your hand, your skin will taste salty. Salt crystals from your swim are sticking to your skin.

Although it is easy to guess that certain substances such as snow, salt, sugar, and diamonds are crystals, it is harder to imagine that aspirin and copper are crystalline or made up of crystals. Yet they are. Scientists had known about crystals for a long time before Dorothy came along. And yet, she was to become famous for her ability to figure out what crystals are like inside or—to put it another way—to find out their internal structure.

A Family Apart

Dorothy was born in Cairo because her English parents had moved to that city so that her father, John Crowfoot, could continue his career. He wanted to be an archaeologist, someone who digs up the remains of ancient civilizations, but there were no jobs in that field then. Instead, he worked in Egypt and the Sudan, where he became director of education. While starting schools in both countries, he also kept in touch with archaeologists. Dorothy's mother, Molly, besides being interested in her husband's work, also collected plants and studied the way both ancient and modern textiles are woven.

In August 1914, World War I began. Molly, John, Dorothy, and Dorothy's two sisters were back in England for the summer. When fall came, Molly and John needed to return to their work abroad, but it was too risky to take the children with them across seas where enemy submarines lurked. Dorothy and her sisters were left in England with a nurse, Katie, in a small house near their grandmother's home. Katie became their adopted mother for the next four years. Only once during the war could Molly make the dangerous journey to see them.

As the war was ending, however, Molly again returned to England, this time bringing with her a new baby, Diana. Because she had been separated from her other daughters for so long, she decided to stay in England with them for a year. Since Molly liked plants, animals, and birds, she taught her daughters about them.

At the end of that year, Molly and John bought a house in England. It was near Beccles, a town in which John's family had lived for generations. During the winter months, while their parents worked abroad, Dorothy and her sisters lived with friends and went to school. For the summer, their mother and father returned to England, and the family was together again in their own home.

When she was eleven, Dorothy began attending the Sir John Leman School in Beccles. By the time she was a teenager, Dorothy was used to taking care of herself. She laughed a lot, and her friends admired her blond hair and blue eyes. Adults thought she was confident, calm, and pretty.

Fascinated by Crystals

Dorothy had always been curious about the materials or substances that make up the things around us and what kind of changes happen when one substance combines with another. The science that tries to solve these puzzles is known as chemistry. Dorothy had first heard about chemistry in a small class she went to in Beccles. There she learned crystals could occur naturally or be produced or "grown" artificially. At the Leman School she was lucky in having a good teacher, Miss Deeley, who made the subject interesting. When, at the age of fourteen, the children selected different subjects for specialized work, Dorothy and one other girl chose to work with the boys on more advanced chemistry.

Dorothy also set up a small laboratory in the attic of her

family's home so that she could do some chemical experiments in her spare time. First of all, she grew crystals as she had been shown how to do in her beginning chemistry class. For instance, beautiful blue crystals can be made by mixing copper sulphate with a small amount of hot water. This solution is then poured into a shallow dish and left for a few days. As the water in the solution evaporates, or changes from a liquid to a gas, the blue crystals are left behind. Other crystals are grown in a test tube or jar, and Dorothy learned how to grow them, too.

No matter how crystals are formed, Dorothy found out, they are alike in certain ways. Every crystal is solid and has a definite, regular shape. Some crystals are shaped like boxes, some like pyramids. They can take other shapes, too, but the units that make up a crystal are arranged in a pattern that repeats itself over and over. Once in a while, when this pattern is repeated without any changes, the crystal is perfect. Many other times changes in the pattern occur, and the crystal is not perfect.

All crystals also have flat sides. Many are so small that they can be difficult to examine even with the most advanced technical equipment. Others can be enormous. Some of the largest known crystals are of a mineral called microcline. What is thought to be a single crystal of microcline weighing 2,000 tons has been found in the Soviet Union.

Besides learning about crystals, Dorothy enjoyed other things she studied in chemistry class. By the time she graduated from Sir John Leman School, she had decided to make chemistry her main subject in college.

By now her mother and father had moved yet again, this time to the city of Jerusalem near the eastern shore of the Mediterranean Sea. Her father had retired from the education department in the Sudan and become a full-time archaeologist, the director of the British School of Archaeology. He and her mother were exploring a number of ancient sites.

Before Dorothy went on to college, she visited her parents and worked with them for a few months while they brought to light the ruins of several churches. She was given the job of drawing the complicated mosaic designs made from small pieces of glass and stones on the floors of the churches. "It was a wonderful experience," she later remembered.

Back in England in 1928, Dorothy began her studies at the University of Oxford. Oxford and other universities are divided into smaller colleges. Each college at Oxford selects its own students and takes care of its own affairs and finances. Many Oxford colleges first attracted students hundreds of years ago. Dorothy attended an all-women's college known as Somerville.

There she became even more fascinated by chemistry and, in particular, by crystals. One of the books her mother had given her when she was sixteen was *Concerning the Nature of Things* by William Henry Bragg. This book was a collection of lectures, mainly for children, given during Christmas vacation from school. In this book Bragg described how X-ray diffraction can be used to discover the structure of crystals. He wrote, "Broadly speaking, the discovery of X rays has increased the keenness of our vision ten thousand times, and we can now 'see' the individual atoms and molecules." Dorothy decided to attend lectures to find out exactly how to "see" atoms through the study of X-ray diffraction.

151

Imagine holding a kitchen strainer—like the ones used to drain spaghetti—so that the beam of light from a flashlight passes through the strainer. The little openings in the strainer will scatter the single light into many small beams. This process is called *diffraction*.

Crystals and everything else in the world, including people, are made of molecules, the basic building blocks of life. These molecules, in turn, are made of atoms. When light shines through the strainer, the pattern of small light beams can be used to show the pattern of holes in the strainer. In the technique Dorothy was learning to use, X rays interact with the regular arrangement of atoms in crystals to give similar diffraction patterns. From the patterns one can learn the structure of the crystals. As the arrangement of atoms becomes more complicated, however, a great many experiments and calculations are necessary to find the structure of the crystals from the diffraction patterns.

At Oxford Dorothy found that among the students there were many more men than women. The women had to follow some rules that seem old-fashioned today. For instance, if a young female student was invited to have lunch with a male student in his on-campus apartment, she had to get permission and be accompanied by an older woman. And, when one of the all-women's colleges decided, for the first time, to allow men to come to their Sunday afternoon teas, the newspapers made a great fuss over the event.

Crystal Research

The strict social rules of the university did not make much difference to Dorothy. She wanted to learn all she could, and that is what she did. Then, in 1932 when she had completed four years of work at Oxford, a lucky opportunity came her way. She was given the chance to work at another excellent English university—the University of Cambridge—with John D. Bernal. He was a well-known scientist who was using the X-ray diffraction technique Dorothy had recently learned.

"In a sense," Dorothy says, "my research with Bernal formed the foundation for the work I was to do during the rest of my career." Under his direction, Dorothy worked on different kinds of crystals, including some of newly isolated vitamins and hormones. Hormones are substances made by our bodies' glands that are carried in our bloodstream to the parts of our bodies where they are needed.

Dorothy was happy at Cambridge, but the people she knew at Oxford hoped she would return to work there. To tempt her, they offered her what was called a "research fellowship." This meant Dorothy received money to live on so that she could spend one more year at Cambridge and then go back to Oxford. In 1934, then, she went back to Oxford, and she has done almost all her work there ever since.

Besides doing research, Dorothy had other duties at Oxford. She tutored in chemistry and soon had the first of a succession of research students. At twenty-four, Dorothy was only a few years older than the men and women she was instructing. In addition, she also was working toward her doctorate degree.

Dorothy was given space for her research in a small room in the university's museum—an old, enormous cave-like building that had skeletons of dinosaurs and whales hanging from the ceiling. Around the walls were collections of dead insects, beetles, and moths. Iron pillars supported the roof, adding to the ghostly atmosphere. It was an odd place for a young chemistry student to have her laboratory.

Dorothy's desk was always covered with piles of scientific papers, letters, articles, and diagrams. It looked completely disorganized, but everyone knew that, if she needed something, she could find it right away.

Important discoveries often begin with much detailed work, and that is how it was for Dorothy. She continued to examine some of the same kinds of crystals she had studied with Bernal at the University of Cambridge. Her work showed she had the qualities a crystallographer—someone who studies crystals—has to have. She was good at mathematics, she gave careful attention to details, and she had a special kind of imagination.

Imagination was, perhaps, the most important quality of all. Indeed, what Dorothy was doing was a little bit like guessing a person's age and weight from fingerprints left on a wall!

Most of us first learn about X rays when a dentist uses them to take pictures of our teeth. The X rays Dorothy used did the same thing they do in a dentist's office—they made images on photographic film. After the X rays she had beamed at thin slices of crystals interacted with the crystals' atoms, the X rays made a regular pattern of dots on photographic film. By examining and measuring the dot patterns, Dorothy was able to figure out the arrangement of atoms within the molecules that made up the crystals. In other words, she discovered the crystals' structure.

Although she was doing complicated things in her laboratory, Dorothy was not at all a solemn young woman. She loved to laugh, and her gentle attention helped her research students achieve exciting results on their projects. Outside of the laboratory she had many friends.

Love and War

In 1937 Dorothy met Thomas Hodgkin, a young man whose family background was similar to hers. For many generations Thomas' family had been made up of historians, doctors, scientists, and writers. Relatives had important connections with the universities at Oxford and Cambridge. Thomas liked to tell jokes and stories. When he was around, people had a good time. He and Dorothy had much in common, and, not long after they met, they were married. That same year Dorothy received her doctorate degree.

During these years everyone in England was aware that a war was likely to start at any time. When it did, in 1939, no one was really surprised. At Oxford, World War II slowly changed things. There were about half as many students as usual, and scientists working at the university were told not to move to other jobs. Nearby, the city of London was the target of German military strength. For their own safety, many people were told to leave the city. Some came to Oxford.

Dorothy's life was changing in many ways. She and Thomas had two children during these war years, a boy and then a girl. Another boy was born in 1946. Partly because everyone contributed what they could to the war effort, Dorothy never thought of giving up her work. "We always had people who were staying with us who could help with the children," she remembers. "And then I think the kind of work I did—the researching and teaching—made it easy to carry on, especially after the children started school."

Studying a Wonder Drug

The war was, in a way, responsible for Dorothy's first big success. Wounded and sick fighting men and women desperately needed a kind of drug that had never been widely used before. Its name was penicillin.

Scientists had known for about ten years that penicillin would grow naturally in small amounts. In fact, that is how it had been discovered. An English professor, Alexander Fleming, had accidentally allowed a speck of a kind of fungus called a mold to drop into a small container in his laboratory. That container held microscopic microorganisms called bacteria. Some bacteria act in ways that are helpful to humans, but others can be deadly. The bacteria in Fleming's container could cause disease.

To his amazement, Fleming discovered that the speck of mold destroyed the bacteria. After he published his findings, two scientists working where Dorothy was, at the University of Oxford, found a way to extract, or take out, penicillin from Fleming's mold. They gave the penicillin to four of eight mice they knew had a disease caused by bacteria. The other four mice did not receive any penicillin. All of the mice that had received penicillin lived; the other four died. Then a few sick people were treated with the new substance. By the time of World War II, though, there was not yet enough available to do any real good.

About this time Dorothy met Ernst Chain, one of the people who had been doing experiments with penicillin. He told her excitedly about his work. He also said he might soon be able to give her some crystals to examine by the X-ray diffraction technique she now knew so well.

Dorothy started work on penicillin with the help of one Somerville research student, Barbara Low. At first, it proved difficult to crystallize penicillin. Finally, in 1943, the first crystals were grown in America and—in the spirit of cooperation during the war—were flown to Dorothy in England. Dorothy and Barbara then grew more crystals of different penicillins, for penicillin can exist in more than one form. Although the penicillin molecule was not very large, it seemed, in those days, complicated, and calculations were slow.

But eventually Dorothy and Barbara, with part-time help from two other investigators, achieved what they wanted. As Dorothy recalls, "We delighted in knowing that we had found the arrangement of atoms in penicillin." Over the coming years their work helped to make it possible for varieties of penicillin and other drugs—which became known as antibiotics—to be produced and combined in large quantities. This development saved lives and changed the history of medicine. Today, penicillin is manufactured in enormous tanks by using a natural fermentation process.

It is hard for us to realize the difficulty of the work Dorothy was doing. The analysis of penicillin spread over two years; it would take perhaps two weeks today. Why did it take so long?

Dorothy's equipment was limited by our standards, and she was not working in what we think of as a modern laboratory. For years, just to reach some special equipment, she had to climb a ladder, holding one of her precious crystals in one hand while clinging to the ladder with the other. Then, too, Dorothy had no computers. They were just beginning to be developed. She and Barbara used hand adding machines until, part way through the war, they were able to obtain a computer that read data by using cards with punched holes. This machine speeded their work.

As part of the work they were doing, special maps were made. These maps were a little like what are called "relief maps"—those that show such features as valleys and mountains on the earth. But the maps Dorothy was working on had to do with crystals. The mountains or "peaks" on her maps revealed where the atoms were within the penicillin molecule. Dorothy had a special talent for interpreting these maps. In a sense, the work that would now be done by a computer was going on in her mind.

Fortunately, for Dorothy, concentration came easily. "She could give all her attention to one of her children's chatter and, in the next moment, be deep in thought about a chemical problem," a coworker remembers. Above all, she was sure that crystal structures that seemed, to others, hopelessly complicated could be understood.

Solving Crystal Mysteries

As crystallographers such as Dorothy began understanding the makeup of crystals, other researchers used this new information to develop a small electronic device that has changed our lives. It is called the transistor.

Transistors are crystals, but they are ones whose molecules are not arranged in perfectly regular patterns. Instead, using the knowledge supplied by crystallographers, the crystals' structure is purposely changed. It is made irregular, or what is called "impure." These impure cyrstals, or transistors, are used in, among other things, computers and television sets. They also make communications satellites possible.

After the war Dorothy moved to a new location in Oxford's museum. A flight of stone steps led up to a long room with windows high above the floor. Here Dorothy and her research group worked. In one half of the room, the young men and women did their research, while Dorothy used the other half. A wall that went partway to the ceiling separated her section from the rest.

Friendly and willing to help, Dorothy was well liked by the research group. When, in the English tradition, work stopped in the afternoon for tea and pastries, she always joined in the conversation. The group was like a big family. Each person was excited not only about what he or she was researching, but also about what the others were doing. Anyone who had a birthday brought in a large iced cake to share.

Soon Dorothy began receiving honors for her work. When she was thirty-seven, she was made a Fellow of the Royal Society of England. This was a great honor for one who was still considered a young scientist and especially for a woman. And it was just one of many that she would receive in the years to come.

One success often leads to the next. In 1948, because he knew of her work on penicillin, Dr. Lester Smith brought Dorothy some special red crystals. They were vitamin B-12 crystals that he had obtained from the liver of animals, and he wanted Dorothy to make them her next project. When she agreed, she opened the door to the unraveling of the most complicated mystery crystallographers had yet solved.

Ever since the 1920s it had been known that people with a certain condition called anemia could improve if they ate special foods, especially liver. People with anemia have less than the normal amount of red blood cells. They may look pale and feel dizzy and sleepy. Since red blood cells carry the oxygen our bodies need, anemia—in its extreme forms—can cause death.

It took quite a few years, however, before investigators learned that it was the vitamin B-12 in liver that helped patients suffering from pernicious (or deadly) anemia. We now know pernicious anemia in humans is caused by a lack of a substance that aids in absorbing B-12 from people's intestines. Today, if people do not have enough of this substance, vitamin B-12 is injected directly into their bloodstreams. That way it does not have to be absorbed from their intestines.

As with penicillin, vitamin B-12 takes a crystal form. Dorothy now had several people working with her on vitamin B-12, and they set out to discover the crystal's structure. This time they had a big advantage.

Powerful computers were available, and Dorothy found a way to use them. One computer was at the University of California at Los Angeles. There, Kenneth Trueblood offered to do calculations for Dorothy on materials she mailed to him. Back and forth information went, from England to the United States and then back again to England. Since Trueblood was teaching classes and carrying on his regular duties during the day, much of his computer work was done at night—many times *all* night—with the help of some assistants.

At one point, Trueblood and his team made a mistake as they were putting information into the computer. Terribly discouraged, he wrote to Dorothy telling her of the hours of calculations that would have to be done over. But Dorothy sent back a telegram saying, "Cheer up." She stayed enthusiastic even when the computer broke down for several months.

In fact, Dorothy never made a fuss when things went wrong. With a casual manner, humming tunes while she worked, she kept making sense of the confusing results of the X-ray diffraction analysis of vitamin B-12. "She went merrily along," an assistant says. Then, too, her memory was known to be excellent. But it was her quiet confidence and humor that made everyone work extra hard on her project.

Dorothy's happy personality was all the more remarkable because, for many years, she had suffered from arthritis. This crippling condition had twisted the joints of her hands into painful and awkward positions. Yet it was with these hands that she skillfully worked with crystals—moving them around in ways no one else could.

After what Dorothy says were "many exciting moments," she and her research group found the structure of vitamin B-12. But it proved very complicated. By a great feat of chemistry, it was later synthesized by a large team led by R. B. Woodward and Albert Eschenmoser. Synthesis is the forming of substances by chemical processes in a laboratory. Fortunately, however, there is an easier way to obtain vitamin B-12 since microorganisms can make it in abundant quantities.

International Trips and Prizes

By this time—the 1950s—Dorothy's family life was changing. Her children were now teenagers. Her husband, Thomas, who had been working in the education field in England, began to take jobs in other countries. Dorothy's work took her to faraway places, too.

China was one of the countries where she went. Although in the 1950s few visitors came to China from Western countries, Dorothy and other English scientists made the trip. Chinese crystallographers and their English guests became friendly and exchanged scientific information. Dorothy also went to the Soviet Union, first in 1953 and then more times in later years.

In 1958 Dorothy and her researchers finally moved

from the old museum where they had continued to work. Their new location was in a modern laboratory in the chemistry building at Oxford. Then, in 1962, Thomas became the first director of African studies at the University of Ghana. By this time, he had become a well-known expert on African history.

Dorothy and Thomas had to make special family arrangements so that they could continue their careers. Along with their three children, they shared a house with one of Dorothy's sisters, Joan, who had five children. Joan, an archaeologist, got a job in Oxford and kept an eye on the eight children when the Hodgkins could not be home. This made it possible for Dorothy to visit Thomas in Ghana for part of his time there. Each summer he came back to England.

And that is how it happened that Dorothy was in Africa in 1964, visiting Thomas, when she learned she had won the Nobel Chemistry Prize. She won the award for finding the structure of important substances by X-ray methods. In particular, her work on penicillin and vitamin B-12 were mentioned as outstanding.

The Hodgkin family, as usual, was spread out all over the world. Dorothy's three children had now grown up and were living and working in different countries. Toby from India and Liz from Zambia came to the award ceremony. Luke in Algeria could not leave his job. He had three children of his own, making Dorothy a grandmother. One of Dorothy's sisters, Diana, was traveling near the North Pole while her husband was near the South Pole. The couple sent a telegram greeting and congratulating Dorothy "from Pole to Pole."

Dorothy received the Nobel Prize and enjoyed the

parties afterwards. The Swedish king talked to her for a long time since they shared the same hobbies. With her usual generous spirit, Dorothy praised "all the other people who worked with me over the years to make this award possible."

Back at Oxford after the excitement, Dorothy knew what she wanted to do. For about thirty years, ever since she had begun her career at Oxford, she had been working with crystals of insulin, a hormone produced in our bodies. But insulin had such a complicated structure that crystallographers—including Dorothy—had not been able to untangle the way it was formed. Not until 1969, after she won the Nobel Prize, did she and her team finally succeed in understanding its structure. Since it turned out that each insulin molecule had 777 atoms, it was not surprising that the research had taken a long time.

Excitedly, Dorothy phoned Max Perutz, an old friend and Cambridge scientist, and told him her results. He made a poster for the Cambridge laboratory that read, "Late night news from Dorothy Hodgkin: Insulin Is Solved." Dorothy's success helped clear the way for other scientists to move toward a better understanding of how insulin works. And, since there is a relationship between our bodies' use of insulin and the condition known as diabetes, Dorothy's work has given a boost to continuing research that may help diabetics.

Other honors besides the Nobel Prize have been given to her. For example, she is a member of the American Academy of Arts and Sciences. One award she is especially proud of is the Order of Merit, which was awarded to her in 1965 by the queen of England. Only one other woman, the famous nurse Florence Nightingale, had won this honor before.

A Lifetime of Excellence

Today, Dorothy is writing about her insulin work in an effort to tie together all the research done over the years. As she has for many decades, she continues to be concerned about the risk of nuclear warfare. Together with other scientists from around the world, she has worked to reduce this threat. The loss of her husband in 1983 has not kept her from visiting friends. When she does, her merry laugh still rings out.

The field of crystallography is changing rapidly. Ever more powerful and faster computers have reduced to minutes the years that calculations used to take to do by hand. In addition, computer graphics make it possible to see a crystal's structure on a screen as it is being worked out. Many substances that are only partly formed of crystals can now be scientifically examined. What is more, crystals can be bombarded with other kinds of energy besides X rays. As more tools are discovered, the X-ray diffraction technique is being used in connection with other methods. By taking photographs with one kind of new microscope, for example, scientists can now look at atoms directly for the first time.

Many women, Dorothy is pleased to see, are interested in the type of work she began. Combining the roles of scientist, wife, and mother is natural to her. She is surprised that anyone would find her life unusual. Yet, she solved difficult problems in a field that was in its infancy. She did it, too, without being outspoken or calling attention to herself except by the excellence of her work.

7.

Mother Teresa

Peace Prize 1979

Standing at the window the small nun, Sister Teresa, looked out over the lawns and gardens of Saint Mary's High School. She was gazing beyond the school grounds to the city streets of Calcutta, India. There, men, women, and children struggled to survive terrible poverty and disease. Sister Teresa felt she belonged in those streets. But, although it was only a few minutes walk from Saint Mary's to the suffering people of Calcutta, she was not yet ready to begin that walk.

As a nun, her first loyalty was to God, to the Roman Catholic church, and to the Sisters of Loreto, the religious group to which she belonged. The Sisters had a hundred-year tradition of service in India. Each time they established a school, they also provided care for orphans and widows. The rules the Sisters obeyed, however, did not allow them to live anywhere except in the convent, a building close to Saint Mary's. On the same large piece of land, the Sisters had several other institutions for girls from different backgrounds. A great many were poor. Students at Saint Mary's learned their lessons in their own language, Bengali.

For seventeen years Sister Teresa taught history and geography in the school's large, high-ceilinged rooms. For a while, she was principal. Her work was interesting and she enjoyed it. But now, in 1946, her life was about to change.

Surrounding Saint Mary's was a district known as a slum. The streets in this slum were the ones Sister Teresa could see from her window. Calcutta had many such areas where people crowded together without enough shelter or food. Women often gave birth right on the street because— since they had no money—there was nowhere else for them to go. Some of these babies lived, but many more were left to die in rubbish heaps. Their mothers could not feed nor care for them. Dirt, rats, and illness were everywhere. Many times no one even noticed when someone died.

Sister Teresa liked working with her pupils and was known as an excellent teacher. Sometimes, though, she thought about moving out from behind the walls of the convent and into the slums to do whatever she could to relieve the suffering she saw. Still, she would never make the decision alone. Her faith was very strong. She was convinced that God would find a way to show her what her next steps should be.

A Religious Childhood

God, Sister Teresa believed, had been guiding her all her life. She had been born in 1910 in what is now Yugoslavia. People of different religions lived in her town, which was called Skopje. Mosques, places of worship for Muslims, and churches for Christians existed side by side.

As a child, Sister Teresa was known as Agnes Gonxha. She did not use the name Teresa until she became a nun.

Agnes lived with her family in Skopje until she was eighteen.

The first ten years of her life were especially happy since she was part of a busy, affectionate family. There was her mother, Drana; her father, Nikola; a sister, Age; and a brother, Lazar. The family's last name was Bojaxhiu. Agnes and Age had good times together, although Age was five years older. Lazar thought Agnes was mischievous and fun-loving. The family was Catholic, and the sisters both sang in the church choir. Since Agnes could sing well, she was given solos to perform. She also played the accordion and the mandolin, an instrument similar to a small guitar.

Agnes' family had a comfortable life and participated in community affairs. Nikola was part owner of a construction company and was involved in politics. Drana was deeply religious and constantly took part in church activities. She also helped needy people in the town. Once, a sick woman had no one to care for her until Drana brought her into the family's home and nursed her until she was well again.

In 1919 Agnes' life changed over the course of a few hours. Without warning, her father felt very ill, was rushed to the hospital, and died in surgery. Suddenly the family had little money. Drana, although used to a comfortable way of life, was not afraid of work and was determined to keep the family together. She established an embroidery business and successfully provided for her children. Agnes and her sister even went to high school at a time when many of the girls in the town did not stay in school that long.

Although the Bojaxhius always had been religious, the Catholic church had an even greater influence on some family members after Nikola's death. "Sometimes," Lazar remembered later on, "my mother and sisters seemed to live *at* church."*

*See note in Suggested Reading.

In addition to regular church services, Agnes attended special religious meetings. Sometimes the leader of these meetings would read letters from faraway missionaries. To Agnes, the lives of these missionaries—people who taught their religion in other countries—were fascinating. One missionary's comment stayed in her mind. "Each person, in life, has to follow his own road," he noted. Agnes began to think that maybe God wanted her to serve him in a special way.

When Agnes spoke to a priest about the possibility of becoming a missionary, he advised her to wait. If she was patient, he said, God would direct her. By the time she was eighteen, Agnes was sure. She learned through her church of a group called the Loreto nuns. Many of these nuns worked in India. When she requested permission to travel to their main convent in Dublin, Ireland, to receive training, she received a reply saying she could come.

Members of her family had different reactions when Agnes told them she was leaving home. Lazar, knowing his sister was a lively person filled with fun, was shocked at her decision. He had just graduated from a military academy and become a lieutenant when he heard the news. He wrote Agnes a letter saying, "How could *you*, a girl like *you*, become a nun?" She wrote back, "You think you are so important, as an official serving the king. . . .Well, I am an official too, serving the King of the whole world. Which one of us is right?"*

Drana was proud of her daughter, but also sad. She knew that young women who left home to become missionary nuns many times did not see their families again. As it turned out, this was indeed the case when Agnes went to Ireland in 1928. Several years later Drana and Age moved to

*See note in Suggested Reading.

Albania to be with Lazar. Their only contact with Agnes over the years was through letters.

Leaving Home to do God's Work

The Loreto nuns Agnes joined chose to follow a certain disciplined way of life. They promised to obey a set of rules. These rules, based on centuries-old beliefs, required that the nuns give up the experiences most young women want so that they could better serve God and Jesus.

Agnes became a nun in training and began to learn English, the language spoken by the Loreto nuns. But she did not stay long in Ireland. Soon the Sisters of Loreto sent her to India where she lived in the city of Darjeeling. There, at the foot of the giant Himalayan Mountains, the Sisters of Loreto had a convent.

In Darjeeling, when she was twenty years old, Agnes made an important step toward becoming a full-fledged nun. She took her first vows. In them she promised to remain in poverty for the rest of her life and never to receive pay for her work. In addition, she could not own many things. All she would be given would be food and a place to sleep. She needed to obey her religious superiors, and she could never marry, in the ordinary sense of the word. Many nuns see themselves as brides of Christ, married to their church.

Agnes now wore the habit, or special long robe and head covering, of the Sisters of Loreto. And she chose a new name, Teresa, to use in her new life. Agnes had in mind Saint Teresa who was known as "the little flower of Jesus." The name attracted Agnes because she was little, barely five feet tall, and because Agnes believed—as had Saint Teresa—that doing everyday, seemingly simple things for people could, over time, make a difference.

While the promises the new Sister Teresa made may seem strict and harsh, she and the other nuns made them willingly and with joy. Sister Teresa believed God was showing her the path he wanted her to follow. Giving up all worldly things was not so hard if you knew God would provide everything you needed. After all, the Bible said, "Look at the birds of the air: they do not sow nor reap nor gather into barns, and yet your Heavenly Father feeds them. Are you not much more valuable than they?" (Matthew 6:26)

Sister Teresa studied, prayed, and learned Bengali and Hindi, languages she would need in India. Soon after taking her first vows, she was sent to Calcutta and began her work at Saint Mary's High School. Although there were sections of the city where the well-to-do had their homes, she was aware that Calcutta also had some of the worst living conditions in the world because of overcrowding, poverty, and lack of food.

Sister Teresa's Call

In 1937 she took what are called final vows and truly became a member of the Sisters of Loreto. For almost twenty years afterward, she worked at Saint Mary's and lived the regulated life of the Sisters. As a teacher, she was loved by her pupils. Then, in 1946 when food supplies failed to reach the school, she went out into the city to try to buy what was needed. The smells of diseased bodies and the sight of beggars lying in the gutters were overwhelming. About a month later, in an unlikely place, Sister Teresa received the message she had been waiting for.

For years, Sister Teresa had been developing the ability to create a quiet space for thinking and praying as she went about her everyday tasks. She no longer needed to be inside a church to communicate with God. And it was while she was traveling on a hot, crowded train from Calcutta to Darjeeling to attend a religious meeting that God commanded her to do something. "I was to leave the convent and help the poor while living among them," she recalls. "It was an order. To fail would have been to break the faith," she continues. The exact way this message reached her is private, she says, a matter between her and God.

Sister Teresa, having heard God's command, could not simply leave the Loreto convent. One of the vows she had taken when she became a nun was that of obedience. Permission to live outside the convent had to be granted by the Catholic church. She went to the head of the church in Calcutta, the archbishop, and told him of her experience on the train. In addition to leaving the Sisters of Loreto, she wanted permission to start a new group or order of nuns— one that would work only with what she called "the poorest of the poor."

The archbishop did not give her permission right away. He had to be convinced that it was truly God's will that she start a new order. Was Sister Teresa really able to do the work she was describing? There were other things to consider as well. India was struggling to become an independent nation. For almost two hundred years, it had been under British rule. Would Sister Teresa, a woman from a European country, be accepted by the Indian people? Then, too, she was a Catholic, while most Indians belonged to the Hindu religion.

It took two years before Sister Teresa received the permission she needed. The head of the Loreto nuns in Ireland was consulted and gave her blessing to the idea. Then Sister Teresa's request was sent on to a representative of the pope in Rome. Finally, in 1948, word came that she could live away from the Sisters of Loreto as an independent nun.

In spite of her eagerness to obey God, the step was not easy. "Leaving Loreto was for me the greatest sacrifice, the most difficult thing I have ever done," she says. "It was a lot more difficult than leaving my family and country to become a nun. Loreto was everything to me."* Sister Teresa continued to remember her years with the Sisters of Loreto as a very precious time. She realized their work—especially the classroom teaching they offered—was an invaluable service to the children of India. And, in the future, she always remained in touch with the Sisters, believing that when she met with them she was truly "home."

Nuns speak of their "vocation," a word that comes from a Latin term meaning "to call." They believe they are called by God to do their particular kind of work. Sister Teresa now felt that God had given her a second call, in a sense a job within a job. She knew this job would be a very difficult one. In order to work with desperately poor and sick people, she would need some nursing training. To get it, she went to stay a few months with the American Medical Missionaries in an Indian city called Patna. These Sisters gave her a temporary home and nursing training free of charge.

Serving the Poor of Calcutta

Returning to Calcutta, she was thirty-eight years old and ready to walk into the slums and stay. Although she insists to this day that she herself is not courageous—and that it is God who gives her all the strength she needs—it was a brave thing to do. She had hardly any money. She was

*See note in Suggested Reading.

not used to living away from her convent, and the streets of Calcutta were frightening. There, human life was threatened in many ways. Unpleasant things could happen to a small woman with no one by her side.

But Sister Teresa had faith. God, she believed, would protect and guide her, both in the ways of the spirit and of the world. Standing in the midst of filth and ugliness, she could smile because she was filled with the certainty that this was where she belonged.

For many months, Sister Teresa worked alone. For a while she spent some time with the Little Sisters of the Poor, a group of nuns who begged for money and then used it to feed and clothe people.

Since Sister Teresa had been a teacher, she was particularly interested in the children of the slums. She began to teach again, but nothing was the way it had been at Saint Mary's. This "school" had no walls, no blackboards, and no chalk or pencils. It was just an open space between huts. She gathered a few children and began to teach them the alphabet by writing the letters in the earth with a stick. More children came.

People began to be aware of what she was doing and some gave her a few pieces of furniture and a little money — enough to buy bars of soap for the children. Their poverty was so great that they had never seen soap. To begin with, Sister Teresa taught them how to clean themselves. She also told them God loved them and had not forgotten them. There could not have been a simpler beginning. Yet Sister Teresa's work was eventually to grow into a movement that would attract hundreds and then thousands of workers.

After some time a friend who was a priest located a good place for Sister Teresa to stay. A man by the name of

Michael Gomes let her have first one room and then more space upstairs in a house he and his brothers owned. He would not let Sister Teresa pay for the rooms, although she offered. The house was on a street called Creek Lane.

Besides working with children, Sister Teresa helped people of all ages who lay in the streets because they were too weak to stand or walk. One day she went to a store with Michael Gomes and showed the manager a list of medicines she needed. She asked that they be given to her free of charge to use for the poor.

"You come to the wrong place, lady," answered the manager. "Let me finish my work in peace." Sister Teresa and Michael Gomes sat down, and Sister Teresa prayed. When she had finished the manager said, "All right, here are three parcels with the medicines you need. You may have them as a gift. . . ."

The Missionaries of Charity

By this time Sister Teresa had been joined by others. The first to arrive was a young woman whom she had taught at Saint Mary's High School. When this young woman took her religious name, she selected "Agnes," since that had been Sister Teresa's name before she became a nun. Then, in 1950, the pope gave Teresa permission to call her group a new religious order.

As head of the order, which she named the Missionaries of Charity, Teresa was now Mother Superior. While the term "Mother" is generally used for the woman who leads a religious order, in Teresa's case it took on even more meaning. She was indeed like a mother to the abandoned people of Calcutta.

Soon more women learned of the work going on in the

slums and came to join. On leaving the Loreto nuns, Teresa also left behind the traditional dress of that order. Instead, she dressed in a simple blue-bordered white sari, draped in the same style worn by Indian women, with a cross pinned to the left shoulder. The women who worked with her also wore these saris. Before long the Missionaries of Charity became a familiar sight in the slums.

Their days were not easy. At 4:30 in the morning they got up, held a worship service, and had breakfast. Mother Teresa made sure they had a balanced diet with enough to eat so that they could do their demanding work and not get sick. After helping in the streets all morning, they returned to the Creek Lane house and had lunch. In the afternoons there was a time for prayers, a short rest, and then more work.

Mother Teresa taught her nuns that, while their work with the poor was valuable, it was meaningless unless it was done with joy. Cheerfulness and love could make even more difference to the people they were helping than food or medicine, she told them. She believed that each time she performed a job like cleaning the sores on a man's face, she was, as she said, "nursing the Lord himself."

Many of the nuns with Mother Teresa were still young, and she knew they needed some time for fun. In the evenings Michael Gomes' house echoed with laughter and shouts as the nuns went out on the rooftop to play games and sing. Then there were prayers and sleep.

But Mother Teresa often worked late into the night in her own room after the others were in bed. She was drawing up the rules her nuns would follow. In addition to the same three vows Mother Teresa had taken when she became a nun, the Missionaries of Charity took a fourth. It was to devote themselves to giving free service to the poorest of the poor.

By this time Michael Gomes' house was overflowing with young women who wanted to be Sisters. The Missionaries of Charity needed a larger place to live. Through the efforts of a priest who enthusiastically supported Mother Teresa's work, and with money lent by the archbishop of Calcutta, a large house with a courtyard was purchased. Over time, Mother Teresa made sure the archbishop was repaid. The new headquarters was on Lower Circular Road.

Even though they now had more room, the Missionaries of Charity kept their promise to live in poverty. They could each have three saris, one to wear while the second was washed and the third dried. Each woman also had a pair of sandals, a bucket for scrubbing, and a thin mattress. "In order to understand and help those who have nothing," Mother Teresa said, "we must live like them." For the same reason, the nuns lived without room fans, even though the temperature in Calcutta could climb above 100°F. And, when someone offered to give them a washing machine, they decided not to accept.

The Home for the Dying

For as long as she had been in Calcutta's slums, Mother Teresa had been especially troubled by the fact that poor people close to death had nowhere to go. For them, doctors and hospitals might as well have been on another planet. Determined to help these desperate people, Mother Teresa decided the Missionaries of Charity were going to open a home for the dying. The health authorities, police, and government officials all heard from her. The nuns prayed every day for God's help.

Then, Mother Teresa was shown a building in the Kalighat district of Calcutta. Dying Hindus came to this district because they wished their bodies to be burned, after death, on the steps of a stream connected with the sacred river Ganges. The building Mother Teresa found had been used as a resting place for worshipping Hindus. Having received permission, she quickly moved in sick patients and nuns to care for them.

At first some people opposed her use of the building, now known as the Home for the Dying. They feared she was trying to make Hindus convert, or change their religion, to the Christian faith. Mother Teresa soon showed by her actions, however, that the Missionaries of Charity would honor each patient's religious beliefs.

At the Home for the Dying, each person follows his or her religious practices. More than half the patients die because they are so ill they cannot be healed. Some of them only want an apple—maybe the first and last they ever see. Others ask a nun to sit by their side for a few minutes.

Mother Teresa does not wait for dying people to be brought to her. She and her nuns go into the streets and look for people who have nowhere else to go. Then, by using cars or old trucks and buses donated to them, the Missionaries of Charity transport these street people to their Home for the Dying. For many it is the only kindness they have ever known. "They live like animals," Mother Teresa observes; "at least they die like human beings."

Children's Home
While walking through Calcutta, Mother Teresa saw babies and children begging for food. Often they only had rags for clothes. Some were crippled or mentally handi-

capped. What could be done to help them?

The answer was Shishu Bhavan, or Children's Home, a two-story building not far from the Missionaries of Charity headquarters in Calcutta. It became a refuge for unwanted infants and children. Gradually, news of this home for children spread. Police, social workers, doctors, and hospitals sent children to Mother Teresa.

Nearly all the children admitted to the home are on the verge of starvation, and most are ill. Every morning at least one Sister goes out to the city's trash bins, often returning with a baby in her arms. Many of the babies die in spite of everything the Sisters can do. Some cling to life and survive, however. These abandoned babies sometimes are smaller than a loaf of bread.

Although they are from the slums, once the children arrive at the home their lives change. In addition to food and medicine, they are loved. The Sisters smile and laugh with them. Many children respond so well to this treatment that, in a few months, no one would guess where they had come from. As soon as the older children grow strong, they are sent to schools. The money to pay the school fees comes from generous people who learn of Mother Teresa's work. Children not mentally capable of attending regular school are taught some handicraft so that they can work.

Some children stay at the home until they are young adults and can marry. Many others are adopted by parents carefully chosen by the Missionaries of Charity. Since Indian families often ask for a child, many of the children can remain in their own country. Families in other nations also have adopted babies and older children from Mother Teresa's home in Calcutta or from the other homes for children she has set up. One of the few possessions she allows herself to have is a collection of photographs sent to her from around the world. These photographs show "her" children smiling happily at the camera with their new parents by their side.

Because the population of India is so large, there are people who think it would be best if there were fewer babies born, particularly among poor people who have difficulty caring for them. Mother Teresa, however, believes that each life is precious. Malcolm Muggeridge, a British broadcaster who interviewed her, observed that—for her—saying there are too many children in the world is like saying there are too many flowers in the fields or stars in the sky.

Children feel Mother Teresa's love. When she comes to visit Shishu Bhavan, they crowd around her, grabbing her sari and calling out her name. She hugs and plays with them. "Aren't they beautiful?" she says, her face glowing.

Sometimes the Missionaries of Charity help children who are living with one of their own parents. If a woman's husband dies, for instance, leaving her with four or five children to support, the Sisters provide funds so that one or two of the children can get some education. That way, when these children grow up, they can find work and take care of the rest of their family.

A Growing Movement

As the years passed, one project led to another. About ten years after the founding of the Calcutta headquarters— and under Mother Teresa's guidance—the Missionaries of Charity opened centers in other cities in India. More money was contributed, including support from the Catholic church. American foods, including milk in powdered form and wheat, were—and are—sent in millions of pounds through Catholic Relief Services and CARE (Cooperative for American Relief Everywhere). Then groups in other countries began writing to Mother Teresa asking her to set up centers. From one Calcutta street the work of the Missionaries of Charity branched out like a strong, growing tree.

In each new location the services offered by the Sisters are those most urgently needed. The nuns run medical clinics, schools, free food distribution centers, and homes for the sick and dying. Such different cities as Addis Ababa in Ethiopia and Washington, D.C., in America have nuns in the same white saris they wear in India working with the poor. What is more, during floods, wars, and other emergencies, the Missionaries of Charity aid those who must leave their homes.

One Christmas in the 1950s, Mother Teresa was having trouble gathering enough toys for the holiday party she always gave for her children in Calcutta. Some people volunteered to collect the needed toys. From this small beginning came an organization that has been of great help to the Missionaries of Charity. It is called the International Association of Co-Workers of Mother Teresa, and it involves people in more than twenty countries. They visit the poor in their homes and in hospitals and prisons and help Mother Teresa's Sisters wherever they are working.

The Missionaries of Charity also encourage the formation of prayer groups all over the world. Mother Teresa believes the support given by these prayers is as important as the good done by contributions of clothes and medicine.

As the movement she had started grew larger, Mother Teresa continued to insist she herself was unimportant to its work. "My life or yours," she once said to an important church official, "it's still just a life."*

Faith, simplicity, strength, and good humor are some of the traits those close to Mother Teresa mention when asked to describe her character. They also point out that she is an excellent manager. Able to make the most of the donations that pour into her headquarters, she often supervises the delivery of materials. For a while, to make sure no supplies were lost or stolen, she rode on top of the carts piled high with rice, reading a prayer book as the cart bounced along.

She prefers not to accept gifts of money from any government, for such grants would mean setting up a complicated bookkeeping system. Her Sisters handle many of the routine details of running the Missionaries of Charity while Mother Teresa is the administrator, making the decisions. Like any good manager of, say, a factory, she can quickly size up a situation and take action. Only in her case, she may be judging a slum and finding out how best to aid the people living there.

Helping the Outcasts

Even with the help the Missionaries of Charity were giving to all kinds of people, Mother Teresa had long been aware that members of one group are treated as outcasts by everyone else. They are called lepers, and their disease is known as leprosy. In 1957 she began to treat lepers in Calcutta by using several ambulances donated to the Missionaries of Charity.

Leprosy has been feared for centuries. Many stories in the Bible mention it as a terrible disease. Until recently there was no way to treat lepers. In an advanced stage, sometimes deformed by losing an arm or leg, lepers can become totally unable to care for themselves. Because those

*See note in Suggested Reading.

who work or live with lepers can contract some forms of the disease, few people are willing to be near a leper. Many times lepers are forced to leave their own homes.

Today, thanks to new medicines, many people with leprosy can be treated. Mother Teresa has opened centers where lepers can come, receive free medicine, and learn how to care for themselves as much as they can. Many lepers are taught to make hammocklike beds and to weave cloth.

Yet Mother Teresa has found that many patients still are not accepted by society, even after they respond to treatment. Often they return to begging on the streets. She thought that they should have homes. On land donated by the Indian government, she built what is really a small town where lepers and their families can live. Here, lepers can learn a trade so that they can support themselves. When Mother Teresa visits this Town of Peace, as it is known, she tells the people there, "God loves you with a special love."

An Avalanche of Awards

In 1962 Mother Teresa received the first in what has been called an avalanche of awards. Once these awards began to be made, people were even more interested in her than they had been before. She still dressed in a plain sari and had the same simple room with a small bed and wooden table. But now her name could be seen by someone reading the front page of a newspaper on the other side of the world.

The award Mother Teresa received in 1962 was the Padmashree Award, and it was given by the Indian government. Since Mother Teresa had been a citizen of India since 1949, the honor came to her from her adopted homeland. The announcement of the award caused a commotion. Catholic church officials wondered if she should accept because nuns were supposed to give up pleasure in things of the world. That was especially true of Mother Teresa and the Missionaries of Charity. Would all the attention be suitable for someone used to living a humble life among the poor?

Finally it was decided Mother Teresa could travel to New Delhi, India's capital, to receive the award. But no one had asked her how she felt, and she decided she did not want to go. It was the Lord's work she had been doing, not her own, she insisted. As she had once said, "I feel like a pencil in God's hand."

The archbishop of Calcutta asked her to come and see him. In their discussion, they found a way around the problem. Mother Teresa would accept the award, not in her name, but in the name of all the sufferers of the world. She was to follow this same policy as she accepted all later honors.

With this award, fourteen years after leaving Saint Mary's High School, Mother Teresa's small face, careworn from years of work, began to appear on television and in news photographs. Millions of people now knew of the work she and her Sisters were doing.

Other honors soon followed. The same year as the Padmashree Award, one of her nuns had a phone conversation with Mother Teresa and told her of the need to build a children's home in Agra, another Indian city. "I told her it was impossible because we had no such money," she remembers. Then the phone rang again. It was a reporter telling her she had just won the Magsaysay Award for International Understanding given by the Philippine government. Along with the award came a sum of money that was exactly the amount needed. "So I called that Sister back to tell her God must want a children's home in Agra," Mother Teresa concludes with a smile.

Over the years, she received more awards from organizations and governments in many different countries. One of the earliest ones came from the United States. It was the John F. Kennedy Award, established in memory of the assassinated Catholic president. Another, given by Great Britain, was the Templeton Prize for Progress in Religion. At the ceremony for this prize, many people were charmed by the sight of Mother Teresa, a tiny, weatherbeaten nun, chatting with Prince Philip, a tall, distinguished member of the royal family.

Especially meaningful was the Pope John XXIII Peace Prize that Mother Teresa received in 1971. She was the first person to receive this award. It was given in the name of Pope John because he sought to bring together the people of the world regardless of their poverty or wealth or the color of their skin. Since Pope John had died in 1963, Mother Teresa accepted the prize from Pope Paul VI in a special ceremony in Rome. As part of the award, she received a sum of money which she used to build a center for lepers. In fact, she has never kept money from any of the awards for herself.

Reaching Out to the World

During the same years Mother Teresa was accepting prizes, she kept working harder than ever. She learned to use jet planes the same way she used a quiet room in Calcutta. Praying, thinking, and planning, she flew to install her nuns in new centers in Australia, the Middle East, and South America. Mother Teresa has visited all the places where her missionaries work around the world. In fact, she has traveled so much that she was given a pass to fly without charge on the Indian airline. Since she has practically no possessions, it takes her only about ten minutes to pack.

As her work expanded, young men began to ask Mother Teresa how they could help. After a small group had come together, the archbishop of Calcutta gave his official blessing to the formation of the the Missionary Brothers of Charity. For the first three years Mother Teresa led the new group as they worked with the poor of Calcutta. After that, a priest known as Brother Andrew became leader of the Missionary Brothers.

More young men joined. They offer medical help and teaching skills. Often they build centers used by the Missionaries of Charity. Though they have helped women, mostly they aid the men and boys of the slums. The Brothers have their own home in Calcutta and, like the nuns, have set up centers elsewhere in India and in other countries.

"I believe in person-to-person contact," Mother Teresa had said more than once. She managed to hold true to that belief in spite of the demands put on her time as the years passed. More gifts came to the Missionaries of Charity. In 1973 a private society gave her a large building in Calcutta, and she promptly filled it with sick people, many of them mentally ill. Never one to waste a minute, she became even better at translating her thoughts into actions. She slept for only a few hours, for she used the nighttime to answer letters that piled up on the table in her room. When sick, she often refused to stay in bed unless a doctor told the Sisters caring for her to make her rest.

Although she did an enormous amount of physical work, hard labor did not change the sharpness of her mind.

Once, the pope presented her with a new car that had been given to him to use on a trip he made to India. Mother Teresa never even thought about taking a ride in her new possession. Instead, she organized a raffle and, by selling chances to win the fancy automobile, made a lot of money to use in her work.

As of 1965 the Missionaries of Charity were honored by being given a special rank that placed the order directly under the guidance of Rome. That high rank was very unusual for a newly formed community of nuns. It made the order known to more people than ever.

Young people joined the Missionaries of Charity in increasing numbers. Businessmen and women volunteered to work in their centers for several hours in the morning before going to work. Children who had never seen starving people heard about what Mother Teresa was doing and found ways to send her contributions. A boy in the United States, for instance, might not buy candy for several weeks, saving the money instead. With this money a child in India could have a drink of milk. With so many people helping, the Missionaries of Charity were able to open homes in most of the world's largest cities, from New York to Tokyo.

As Mother Teresa and her nuns came to know life in Western countries, they realized poverty can exist in many forms. As Mother Teresa says, "People are not hungry just for bread, they are hungry for love." Sometimes she finds what she calls "poverty of the spirit" inside wealthy people's homes. One elderly man told Mother Teresa that her nuns were the only visitors he and his wife ever had. The couple had more than enough money, but what they needed could not be bought. Young or old, rich or poor, the worst disease for anyone, Mother Teresa finds, is being unwanted.

Against her wishes, Mother Teresa became famous. Her picture even appeared on the cover of *Time* magazine. Still, wherever news of her traveled, it was noted that she remained true to her beliefs and to the vows she had taken. Presidents, kings, and entertainers, she met them all, but she still was most comfortable with the plain people of poverty. From them, she says, she learns about love.

One story she likes to tell is about a family with eight children. Hearing that the family was starving, Mother Teresa brought rice. She says she saw the children's eyes "shining with hunger." The mother of the family took the rice and divided it, keeping only a portion for her own children and herself. The rest she took to the family next door who also had nothing to eat. The woman was a Hindu, and her neighbors were Muslims, but their religion made no difference, Mother Teresa points out. The joy of sharing, she observes, can take place even when there is only a cup of rice.

"I Accept in the Name of the Poor"
It is a long flight from the streets of Calcutta to Oslo, Norway. One day in December 1979, Mother Teresa climbed down the steps of a plane after making that trip. In her sari and sandals, with only a short coat around her in the cool air, the little nun had come to receive the Nobel Peace Prize. What a long way she had traveled, not only in miles, but in what she had accomplished.

Mother Teresa, of course, did not feel she herself had won the prize. When she learned of the Nobel committee's decision, she said, "Personally I am unworthy. I accept in the name of the poor because I believe that by giving me the prize they've recognized the presence of the poor in the world." The members of the Nobel committee who had

189

voted to give her the award also recognized that hunger and poverty can help bring about wars. By fighting these causes of trouble, Mother Teresa had contributed to world peace.

The first evening after arriving in Oslo, she was greeted by a parade of people carrying torches that sparkled in the night. Her brother, Lazar, and her niece came to Oslo to be with her. Lazar was very proud of the woman he still thought of as his little sister. All through the speeches, ceremonies, and other festivities that followed, Mother Teresa remained, as always, modest and quiet.

Nobel winners traditionally are given a banquet. Mother Teresa asked that the dinner in her honor be cancelled so the money that would have been spent could be given to the poor. The Nobel Foundation agreed and presented her with a check for $7,000. Moved by her down-to-earth manner and simplicity, the Norwegians had a "People's Collection" to raise donations for her work. The Nobel Prize itself carried with it $190,000, an amount Mother Teresa used to build more homes for the poor and suffering people of the world. A sizable portion was used to help lepers.

Often the Nobel Peace Prize has gone to politicians. In 1979 many people were happy to see it awarded to someone who had stayed away from anything to do with politics or national differences. Mother Teresa belonged to the world, not to any one government or country. The people of India, however, certainly could not be blamed for taking special pride in her work.

Mother Teresa made clear in Oslo, as she had elsewhere when she received prizes, that God was working in the world through her. She herself was unimportant. Her faith gives her a special radiance, and those who saw her in Oslo remember the warmth shining in her eyes.

When she stood to give her Nobel speech, she was surrounded by a sea of people wearing dark clothes. Since it was December, the audience was formally dressed in winter colors. Her figure, in its white sari, seemed to be a pinpoint of light in the large hushed room. Near the end of the speech she said, "And so let us always meet each other with a smile, for the smile is the beginning of love. . . ." That day in Oslo a lot of people smiled back at Mother Teresa.

Like most Nobel winners, Mother Teresa found that the award made life even busier than it had been before. Invitations to attend special events and to accept honorary college degrees were delivered to the Missionaries of Charity's home in Calcutta. For a while she accepted many of the invitations. In 1980 India presented her with its highest honor, the Jewel of India Award. Mother Teresa said she received this prize on behalf of all men and women who had dedicated themselves to helping the poor and suffering all over India. She also said she accepted in the name of all religions.

One Person Can Make a Difference

At the same time her work expanded at an amazing rate. The year she won the Nobel Prize, she opened fourteen centers outside of India. India itself now had more than a hundred centers. Each morning the Missionaries of Charity were feeding more than seven thousand people in Calcutta alone.

Even as Mother Teresa's work was praised, it also was being criticized. Even though people realized how hard she worked, some thought the needs of the poor of the world were so great that the Missionaries of Charity could never make enough of a difference. These critics wanted to change society itself, to do away with the causes of poverty and disease.

Mother Teresa understood how they could feel this way. But she remained convinced that God had chosen her to serve in a particular way. She would keep on working, knowing those she reached were far better off than if she had never found them. Looking at a crowd of people, she was able to think about helping each individual, instead of becoming overwhelmed by the combined problems of the whole group.

Gradually, Mother Teresa came to feel she had to limit the time she spent away from her work. She discouraged members of the press from interviewing her and, since she found it difficult to give speeches, she did not give them whenever possible. Now she left the poor people only when she felt she must. One of these times occurred when Pope John Paul II was shot in May 1981. She flew to visit him as he lay wounded in a Rome hospital.

On a trip to the United States in the same year, she opened a center in a Spanish-speaking neighborhood of Newark, New Jersey. Like all of the homes run by the Missionaries of Charity, this center was staffed by nuns from different countries. The Newark workers were from India, the Philippines, and America. They began their work by visiting patients in hospitals and prisoners in local jails. Mother Teresa also opened a home in Washington, D.C. While she was there she was invited to the White House where she met President Ronald Reagan.

The next year, during another United States visit, Mother Teresa opened her first American home for the poor in a rural area. This home was in a mountainous part of Kentucky where hardly any of the people were Catholic.

To Mother Teresa, all that mattered was that poor people needed the work her nuns could do.

On this same trip Mother Teresa spoke to the graduating class of Harvard University. During the ceremony, there was a special moment. Some of the children who had been adopted by families in the United States held up a big sign they had made. It said, "Hello, Mother Teresa, from your kids." The children ran up to the stage and hugged the little nun. Several were interviewed by reporters. They said they had loved her from the first time they met her in Calcutta.

In August 1982, Mother Teresa traveled to war-torn Lebanon to visit her Sisters in Beirut. While she was there she went to a children's hospital that had been hit many times by shells and rockets. There was no water and little food. In addition to their physical problems, many of the children were not of normal intelligence.

A Red Cross official who saw what happened next says, "Mother Teresa fell to her knees and prayed for a few seconds. The next thing we knew she was rattling off a list of supplies she needed. . . ." Mother Teresa had decided to move the children to a place of shelter run by the Missionaries of Charity in East Beirut. She carried many of the children to safety in her own arms.

Visitors to her order in Calcutta quickly see the special bond between Mother Teresa and her nuns. When she visits one of her Indian homes, the Sisters are overjoyed to see her. When she leaves they say, "Come back soon, Mother. God bless you."

The nuns tell many stories of the kindness Mother Teresa has shown them. One chilly night the Missionaries of Charity were opening their center in Melbourne, Australia.

The Sisters gave a few extra blankets to Mother Teresa because she had recently broken her arm, and they wanted her to rest it on the folded blankets. After seeing Mother Teresa settled, the Sisters went to sleep. In the morning they found the blankets had been spread over them during the night.

Why is Mother Teresa welcomed wherever she goes? Perhaps in a world where it seems only large corporations or powerful governments control the course of events, people hunger for an individual who makes a difference. With Mother Teresa's work as an example, people can still say, "See, each human life is valuable."

Since she is no longer young and, as she puts it, someday will go home to God, Mother Teresa has written into the rules of her order a way her nuns can elect a new leader. She often has said she hopes the woman who takes her place will be the least likely of her Sisters. That way, she thinks, everyone will understand that it has been God's work all along and not hers.

For now, each day, she continues to go wherever a sick person waits, a child cries in hunger, or a poor person lives in despair. No walls can stop her love.

8.

Barbara McClintock

Physiology or Medicine Prize 1983

Early in the morning a short slim woman enters her laboratory in Cold Spring Harbor, a small town on Long Island in
New York State. She moves quickly to begin her day's research and, except for her wrinkled face, few people would
guess she is over eighty years old. When more researchers
arrive, Barbara McClintock already has been working for
several hours. In another part of the building a phone rings.
The caller, a reporter, says, "I'd like to set up a time to
interview Dr. McClintock for an article I'm writing on
famous women scientists." "I'm sorry," the Cold Spring
Harbor staff member replies, "Dr. McClintock hardly ever
gives interviews."

While Barbara McClintock is a very private person, a
small group of men and women have been her friends for
years. To them, she has to make no explanation of her
feelings or her unusual scientific approach. They know she
lives her life the way she wants to live it.

She does not own a phone or a house, although she can

afford them. For a large part of her career, Barbara has shunned the time-consuming meetings and classroom teaching many scientists feel they should include in their schedules. That way she can concentrate on the kind of scientific work she wants most to do. This disciplined effort, coupled with the keenness of her intelligence, has put her in the forefront of her field.

Growing Up Independent and Strong Willed

A combination of Barbara's own personality and way of thinking, along with events early in her career, started her down a path few scientists have followed. From childhood she seems to have been independent and strong willed. The third of three daughters, Barbara was born in Hartford, Connecticut, in 1902 to Sara and Thomas Henry McClintock. A fourth child, a son named Malcolm Rider but called Tom, was born a year and a half later. The family did not have much money for a number of Barbara's growing-up years because it took a while for her father to establish himself in medical practice. A little more than a year after Tom's birth, Barbara was sent to live with an aunt and uncle in Massachusetts. She stayed with this couple on and off until she reached school age.

Barbara had a good time when she was in Massachusetts. Her uncle was a fish dealer, and she was allowed to ride with him in a horse-drawn carriage while he sold his fish. In fact, the men in her family had a strong influence on her. At various times she helped both her uncle and her father repair different kinds of machines.

In 1908 the McClintocks moved to Brooklyn, a borough of New York City. There Barbara, her sisters, and brother attended elementary school and then Erasmus Hall High

School. At that time the part of Brooklyn they lived in still had woods and open fields to play in. The family spent many summer days at Long Beach, which was then a Long Island summer resort within easy traveling time for city residents. Here, Barbara learned to swim and took long walks along the beach with just the family's dog for company. In fact, she liked to be alone and often sat reading and thinking for hours at a time.

Evelyn Fox Keller, author of a biography on Barbara, observes that, in the McClintock family, school was only one of the things considered important for a child's education. Barbara's father even went to his children's school and insisted that they were not to receive any homework. He thought the instructors should be able to teach them what they needed to know during regular school hours. Each McClintock child was encouraged to develop his or her own special talents. When Barbara's parents noticed she liked to ice skate, they bought her the best skates they could find so that she could go ice skating in Brooklyn's Prospect Park.

Barbara often played street games with her brother and his friends. She also climbed trees and spent much time out-of-doors. She remembers being the only girl she knew who did these things. In the early years of this century, most city girls were expected to spend any spare time at home, quietly sewing or reading.

Many weekends Sara took her children sightseeing in different parts of New York City. Before they went she told them about what they were going to see. Once, a trip to the Statue of Liberty was planned. "The Statue is 152 feet high, you know, children," Sara said. "That's no problem, Mother," Barbara replied. "I can shinny up!"

By the time she was a teenager, Barbara had discovered

she liked to learn about all sorts of things. Always an enthusiastic reader, she first discovered science at Erasmus Hall High School. She enjoyed trying to solve the problems given to her class and often found solutions different from the answers her teachers expected.

When World War I began, Dr. McClintock was sent overseas as a military surgeon. The family once again had financial worries. Sara, who had been giving piano lessons, took on more pupils. During these years one of Barbara's older sisters received a scholarship to college. She decided not to accept it, though, for in those days many people thought that if a young woman earned a degree young men might think she was too smart to make a good wife. When Barbara reached college age, however, she was determined to continue her education.

Although, at the time, the McClintocks were quite poor, Barbara's parents understood her feelings. Her father was still overseas, and the fall term at college was just months away. To help the family's finances, she took a daytime job at an employment agency. But she continued her studies on her own at night.

A High-Quality Education

By the summer of 1919, Barbara knew which college she wanted to attend. It was Cornell University in Ithaca, a town in the rolling hills of upstate New York. At this time, Cornell—more than most other coeducational universities—was committed to giving women as well as men a high-quality education. Barbara wanted to enroll in Cornell's College of Agriculture, whose graduates were respected leaders in their professions. Although she still had no thought of actually having a career, she knew courses in the kinds of things she wanted to study were available at Cornell.

That fall, just after her father returned to America, Barbara managed to register at Cornell. She never was sure exactly who made it possible. All she cared about was that she was where she wanted to be.

College turned out to be everything Barbara had expected. In contrast to her younger years when she often had spent hours alone, she now made many friends among both the young men and women at Cornell. Not long after arriving, she was elected president of the women's freshman class.

Although she had enjoyed mathematics and physics in high school, it was at Cornell that she truly became interested in science. In her junior year she was singled out as having special talent. A professor invited her to take a graduate-level science course even though she did not yet have her bachelor's degree.

Outside the classroom Barbara sometimes did things that surprised other people. One day she had her long hair cut in a short easy-to-care-for style. Many of the other students commented on her new hairdo, not all in a complimentary way. Within a few years a similar style became popular with women all over the United States—Barbara had just cut hers a little sooner.

She took great pleasure in music as well as science. In her senior year, Barbara played the banjo in a jazz group that performed in student gathering places.

After receiving her bachelor of science degree in 1923, she became a full-fledged graduate student. Since the plant breeding department—the one Barbara wanted to join— would not accept graduate women, she registered as a student of the botany department.

Discovering Genetics

The courses Barbara was especially interested in were those on genetics. Genetics is the scientific study of heredity. And heredity is defined as the passing on of characteristics from parent to offspring. The units of inheritance are known as genes, and it is genes that in humans, for instance, largely determine how tall we are as well as the color of our hair and eyes.

But plants, insects, and other living things also have genes, and Barbara was interested in the genetic study of a particular kind of plant—corn. The corn she learned about is called maize, or Indian corn. Maize often is used to make autumn decorations. The reason it makes an attractive decoration is the same reason it is used by those studying genes. An ear of maize can have kernels that are many different colors, and even an individual kernel can be speckled or streaked. Maize leaves also have varying color patterns. By studying generations of these plants, scientists called geneticists learn how the colors are inherited.

In the mid-1920s when Barbara was becoming fascinated by the subject, genetics was still a young science. Its growth dates from 1900 when three scientists, working independently of each other, performed experiments that proved the accuracy of the earlier work of Gregor Mendel. Mendel, an Austrian monk who lived from 1822 to 1884, experimented with pea plants in the garden of his monastery. Through his work and painstaking record keeping, he discovered the basic laws of heredity. During his lifetime, however, the importance of what he had found was not recognized.

When the scientific community accepted Mendel's conclusions at the turn of the century, modern genetics was born. It took a while before what Mendel had called "factors" were named "genes" and even longer for researchers to prove that genes were real. At first scientists only guessed at their existence. But evidence continued to suggest that genes were carried on chromosomes—microscopic rod-shaped bodies inside the cells of living things.

In the ten-year period before Barbara came to Cornell, a noted geneticist—one who specialized in the study of maize—was working at the university. The investigations of this man, Rollins Emerson, pushed forward what was known about the inherited characteristics of corn. At the same time, however, at Columbia University in New York City, another geneticist, Thomas Hunt Morgan, was working with the fruit fly, *Drosophila melanogaster.* His famous experiments revealed a great deal of new information about inherited traits.

Geneticists who worked with fruit flies had advantages over those working with maize. A new generation of fruit flies can be produced every ten days while—at least in most parts of the United States—only one crop of corn can be grown a year (without using a greenhouse). Even more importantly, though, more was known about fruit fly chromosomes than about those in maize. In particular, it was possible to distinguish one chromosome from another. In maize, on the other hand, while chromosomes had been seen under a microscope and even counted, no one had yet learned how to tell them apart.

Understanding Maize

When she was just a graduate student, Barbara revolutionized maize genetics by identifying the individual members of the set of chromosomes within each cell. She taught herself to distinguish each of the ten chromosomes in maize by comparing structure and length. Her discoveries made it possible for maize geneticists to stop relying only on the characteristics of corn they could observe with their naked eye. They now had the ability to make careful microscopic comparisons of maize chromosomes over several generations.

From 1924 to 1931, Rollins Emerson's research group—of which Barbara was a member—did pioneering work in maize genetics. Although at this time most women in science were technicians or teachers, Barbara now knew she wanted to be a research scientist. Having received her master's degree in 1925, she continued on to obtain her doctorate in 1927. By chance, another young woman who was later to win a Nobel Prize, Pearl Buck, also was studying at Cornell during the mid-1920s. It is, however, unlikely that the two met, since one was studying literature and the other science.

During these years Barbara enjoyed her research and became friendly with many of the researchers with whom she was working. About the time she got her Ph.D., a young graduate student, Marcus Rhoades, came to Cornell. He and Barbara formed an immediate friendship. Rhoades was enthusiastic about her efforts to map the location of certain genes on maize chromosomes—genes that controlled particular inherited traits.

Between 1929 and 1931 Barbara published articles in scientific journals that gave the details of her work. Each article was considered by others in her field to be a major contribution. She exchanged ideas with Marcus Rhoades and another young scientist, George Beadle, both of whom were doing the same kind of research. The trio felt they were making excellent progress toward understanding the secrets of the genetic makeup of maize.

During these years Barbara also worked with a woman, Harriet Creighton. A recent graduate of Wellesley College, Creighton came to Cornell in 1929. She and Barbara became good friends. In the late afternoon, after work was over in the laboratory, they played tennis. Together, Harriet Creighton and Barbara made a discovery that even today is considered a milestone in the development of the field of genetics. In 1931 they published their findings. Their experiments proved that the exchange of genetic information that occurs during meiosis, or cell division for reproduction, is accompanied by an exchange of chromosomal material. Before their research, no one knew for sure that this was true.

The nature of Barbara's work required that she closely observe each generation of maize plants she wanted to use. She and her coworkers had to plant and then painstakingly care for their corn. Most importantly, they had to make sure that pollination, the process by which corn reproduces, took place the way they wanted.

Corn usually pollinates itself through the action of wind, when pollen falls from the corn tassel and settles on a part of the corn ear called the silk. Corn geneticists cannot allow this process to happen by chance. For their purposes, only certain pollen must come in contact with certain silks. Geneticists prevent accidental pollination by tying paper bags over the ears of corn before the silks appear. Then they collect the pollen they want to use by enclosing the appropriate tassels in a different set of bags. Finally, they pollinate by hand according to a prearranged plan. This way they can control the breeding process and obtain ears of corn for which they know the genetic makeup.

An Independent Researcher

In this same year, 1931, Barbara decided it was time to leave Cornell. No proper academic appointment had been offered her, even though she had been at the university for twelve years and had held the title of instructor since receiving her doctorate degree. Looking for a way to continue her research, Barbara was glad to accept a fellowship from the National Research Council. This position gave her a means of support for the next two years. She divided her time between the University of Missouri and the California Institute of Technology.

At the University of Missouri, Barbara worked with Lewis Stadler, another scientist fascinated by maize. Barbara focused her research on the mutations, or changes, in maize plants brought about by deliberately bombarding them with X rays. This was a process in which Stadler was a pioneer.

During the summer of 1931 at the University of Missouri, Barbara examined what she called ring chromosomes. These ring chromosomes accounted for different patterns of colors that she could see in corn plants Stadler had planted for her in Missouri that spring. This knowledge was to prove valuable to her in her later work.

At the California Institute of Technology—known as Cal Tech — she was the first woman to hold the position of postdoctoral fellow. She became part of a team of geneticists in the division of biology. This group was put together by the same Thomas Hunt Morgan who had begun revolutionary experiments with fruit flies as early as 1910.

A coworker from Barbara's California days, James Bonner, remembers having long discussions with her as they both worked far into the night. In a Cal Tech publication he later recalled that Barbara had told him "she had met only two men worth having as husbands—both of them geneticists—and that since neither was available, she planned to remain single."

As part of a friendly group at Cal Tech, Barbara went to picnics and on trips to beaches and mountains. She was now thirty years old and every day more dedicated to her research. In order to move easily between the laboratories at Cal Tech and the University of Missouri—and once in a while to return to Cornell where she still planted corn crops—Barbara bought her first automobile, a Model T Ford. She enjoyed being independent.

In 1932 the Sixth International Congress of Genetics took place in Ithaca, New York. Geneticists from all over the world heard Rollins Emerson praise Barbara's work in his speech on maize genetics. Barbara served as vice-chair of one of the Congress' meetings and delivered a paper on her chromosome work. By this time she was recognized as a leading maize geneticist.

The following year she received a Guggenheim Fellowship to go to Germany. This was an honor that—in normal circumstances—she would have benefited from greatly. However, 1933 was a bad time to travel to Germany. Barbara expected to work with geneticist Richard Goldschmidt, but her research never really got started.

Even though Barbara was not Jewish, she had had many Jewish friends in college. She was upset when she arrived in Germany and saw the influence Hitler and his political party had in the country. This influence was growing stronger daily and would soon have disastrous results for Jewish people. Many German Jews, afraid of what the future held, were beginning to seek ways to flee their homeland.

Struggling to Find a Real Job

Shaken, Barbara returned to Cornell to find the United States in the midst of the Great Depression. Jobs were hard to find, her fellowship from the National Research Council had ended, and she had to find a way to support herself. In spite of the poor economic situation in America, she might have been able to find a teaching job. Yet she was determined to remain in a laboratory as a research scientist.

She realized quite suddenly she had a career—something she had never really thought about before. Surely, she thought, with the scientific reputation she had made, there must be a place for her in a university.

Through the efforts of Rollins Emerson and Thomas Hunt Morgan, Barbara received a grant from the Rockefeller Foundation. The grant was then renewed so that she was ensured a place in Emerson's laboratory. However, more and more she resented the difference between the treatment her male coworkers received and her own.

The men with whom she had shared the adventure of being a young, hard-working graduate student now had positions that guaranteed them a good salary and the hope of later moving into even better positions. Many held jobs at universities. Barbara was just as intelligent as the men and had brought about as many or more scientific advances. Still, her career seemed to progress in fits and starts while theirs moved smoothly along. While the male scientists she knew respected her knowledge and treated her fairly, their respect did not give her the same long-range security they enjoyed.

Finally, Lewis Stadler, with whom she had worked before, secured a position for Barbara as associate professor at the University of Missouri. It was her first offer of a faculty position and, in 1936, she accepted with relief.

Over the next five years, her career reached a high point. In a series of articles, the first of which was published in 1938, she reported on ways chromosomes could break apart and then join together in new combinations. Then, in 1939, she was elected vice-president of the Genetics Society of America.

After teaching at the University of Missouri until 1941, Barbara decided to leave. One reason for her decision may have been that the budget for her department was reduced. Barbara had no advance warning about the budget cut. Now she was without a job at a time of national crisis. In a few months the United States would enter World War II. But, since the genetics field was not essential to the war effort, the conflict did not provide work for her as it did for many other women.

Above all, Barbara needed a place to grow her corn so that she could have a new crop to study. She wrote to her old friend Marcus Rhoades who had just taken a new position at Columbia University in New York City. Rhoades was going to plant his corn at Cold Spring Harbor, Long Island, about forty miles east of Manhattan. At this site there was a department of genetics supported by the Carnegie Institution of Washington, D.C.

A Scientific Home
Barbara decided to try to plant her corn there, too. She wrote to another old friend, Milislav Demerec, a geneticist already working at Cold Spring Harbor. He said she was welcome to come. She went in June, not realizing that for more than the next forty years she would make Cold Spring Harbor her home.

Soon after she arrived Demerec became the director of

the Cold Spring Harbor Department of Genetics. He promptly offered Barbara a one-year position, which she accepted. A few months later he suggested making the position permanent. The offer was hard to decline. Cold Spring Harbor gave her a place to grow her corn, a laboratory, a place to live, and a salary. She agreed to stay, thus beginning an association with the Carnegie Institution that would give her both the support and freedom she desired.

Cold Spring Harbor had a small group of year-round researchers, but in the summer its population suddenly grew much larger. During that season scientists and their families came from other parts of the country and from abroad to relax on nearby beaches. While they were there, they spent time working in laboratories and talking over their research with one another. When fall came, however, the visitors went back to their regular jobs, and Cold Spring Harbor became a small community again.

Because the Cold Spring Harbor staff was small, each researcher pursued his or her own work. Besides Barbara, no other maize geneticist worked at the laboratory on a permanent basis. Nevertheless, she talked with other researchers and kept in touch with coworkers when she attended scientific meetings and lectures. She also read about developments in genetics in scholarly journals and papers.

During the same decade Barbara came to Long Island, events were occurring that rechanneled genetic studies into a new area. In fact, many of the scientists involved in these changes did part of their work at Cold Spring Harbor. Genetic researchers began to concentrate on unraveling the secrets of heredity by understanding the basic chemical makeup of genes and chromosomes.

Since the new area of study concentrated on the way

molecules are arranged in living cells, it came to be known as molecular biology. Researchers already knew that nucleic acids, substances found in chromosomes, play an important role in storing and passing on hereditary information. Now, investigation of one type of nucleic acid, which came to be known as DNA—an abbreviation of its name, deoxyribonucleic acid—answered many of the fundamental questions of genetics.

Not too far in the future, newspaper articles would announce each exciting step taken by molecular biologists. The investigations of maize geneticists, on the other hand, would be thought of as old fashioned and treated as if they were of little importance. In fact, the two lines of research fitted together, but no one as yet understood this connection.

During the three years after she arrived at Cold Spring Harbor, Barbara made a great deal of progress in her work. She published her results in the annual reports of the Carnegie Institution and in an article for *Genetics*, the journal where geneticists frequently announce their discoveries.

Planting and raising corn each year had its challenges. One kind of challenge appeared at night, had a black mask, four feet, and a bushy ringed tail. These invaders were raccoons, and they liked corn as much as Barbara. Unfortunately for her experiments, though, the coons wanted to feast. To protect her precious harvest, she often took a sleeping bag and camped out in her corn field, waking up once in a while to shoo the trespassers away.

The year 1944 turned out to be a very good one for Barbara. She was elected president of the Genetics Society of America and also became a member of the National Academy of Sciences—only the third woman in the history of this professional society to receive the honor.

In addition, she went on a visit to see George Beadle, her friend from Cornell days. Beadle, who was now at Stanford University in California, invited Barbara to solve a problem he was having in his investigation of the chromosomes of a red mold, *Neurospora*. In the short time she spent at Stanford, she made astounding progress. Not only did she count and identify the chromosomes, but she was able to track them through the entire meiotic cycle. During this cycle, through cell division, the number of chromosomes in reproductive cells is reduced to half the original number.

"*Jumping Genes*"

Although it would not be evident right away, the most important development of the year occurred when Barbara returned to Cold Spring Harbor. There she began experiments that would be the most challenging of her career.

By this time she had been observing maize plants for about a quarter of a century. These years of experience were the single best aid to her research. The powerful tools that exist today, such as the electron microscope, were not available then. But she had keen eyes—eyes that did not miss much of what happened over the generations of maize she raised and studied. The molecular biologists sought to simplify the science of genetics by reducing it to a series of chemical building blocks. Barbara, though, was not afraid to see the hereditary process in all of its parts.

She started by looking even more closely at the way the kernels on corn cobs and the leaves on corn plants are colored or pigmented. This was more of the same type of observation she had been doing for years. By looking carefully, certain pigmentation patterns could be found. These patterns usually stayed the same within the life cycle of a particular corn plant. In other words, the patches of color on the kernels and leaves tended to be passed on faithfully. The differences in color represented mutations, or inherited changes, in the chromosomes within the plant's cells.

Barbara reasoned that there could not be such sameness in the color patterns unless something within the plant's chromosomes was regulating or controlling the rate of mutation. Soon she took this idea another step. She found that occasionally there were exceptions. That is, sometimes a part of a plant—a section of a leaf or ear—showed a rate of mutation that differed from that of the plant as a whole. She decided to follow this one clue and see where it led her.

For six more years she did her research and finally reached the point where she thought she understood what was happening. Her answer, she believed, was the only one that explained the changes she saw. The fact that her findings challenged what geneticists had believed for years did not bother her.

At that time geneticists assumed that genes were arranged on chromosomes like pearls on a necklace. Above all, they believed, genes did not move. Barbara's conclusions were revolutionary beause they suggeseted that genes *did* move, and that they could shift positions on chromosomes. What was more, when they moved or "jumped" they caused some very exciting things to happen.

To put it simply, Barbara discovered that some genes, which she labeled DS (dissociation elements) would "jump" from one part of a chromosome to another if they were "signaled" to do so by an AC gene (or activator element). When a DS gene jumped, it would then influence the genes that were its new neighbors. If the DS gene happened to move next to a gene that determined the color of a corn kernel, the DS gene would suppress, or "turn off," that gene. Then the kernel would be a paler color than it otherwise would have been. If the DS gene moved again, the gene determining color could regain its normal function. According to Barbara, the AC genes were acting like switches, turning "on" and "off" the genes that determined the colors she could see on her ears of corn.

Transposition was the term Barbara used to describe this process. She called the genes she observed "controlling elements," but they later came to be known as "jumping genes." While she expected it would be difficult to convince other geneticists of the truth of what she had discovered, she was willing to try. After all, her friend Evelyn Witkin, another Cold Spring Harbor researcher, could understand her observations.

Barbara carefully gathered her data. She wanted to be able to answer all the questions she expected to hear when she presented her ideas publicly at the Cold Spring Harbor Symposium in the summer of 1951. Surely geneticists at this meeting, she thought, would realize transposition opened the door to marvelous possibilities.

Unfortunately, Barbara had some difficulty in presenting her observations. In the hour's time she had for her talk, she gave so much information so quickly, in a kind of verbal shorthand, that her listeners were overwhelmed. When she finished, no questions were asked.

The theory of controlling elements was revolutionary. Because there was only a small number of maize geneticists, few investigators could immediately appreciate Barbara's findings. Still, there were some who did. Later, after she put her observations in written form, the information was there for those who wanted to take the time and make the effort to understand it.

Fighting for Acceptance

Above all, Barbara was known for the precision of her work. Most other geneticists continued to respect, if not endorse, her point of view. During the 1950s she used her own well-developed intellectual powers and went on working harder than ever. She was willing to let her work speak for itself.

In 1947 the American Association of Univerity Women had recognized her work by presenting her with an Achievement Award. The association's journal carried an account of the award ceremony and of the remarks she made at the time. Speaking of the role she thought women would play in scientific research in the coming years, Barbara had pointed out that women might consider a career in research in order to have an equal chance with men. She said, "A purely research position will not be subject to the discriminatory forces that a position in administration or teaching might produce. A woman will be able to enter such a position with confidence—a factor that must not be neglected if she is to do her best work."

This was exactly the kind of confidence Barbara herself needed at this time in her life. Since she was not a member of a research group or working at a university with other maize geneticists, she had no one who could step in and explain her ideas to others in her field. The explanations she did offer were found mainly in the Carnegie Institution's Annual Reports. Scientists were not used to looking at such reports to find out the details of current research.

By the 1950s the molecular biology revolution was in full swing. In 1953 James Watson, an American, and Francis Crick, an Englishman, proposed a structure for DNA. DNA, they said, consists of two intertwined strands that are coiled in a double helix—a structure that somewhat resembles a spiral staircase. What was more, these investigators suggested the way DNA copies itself and transfers genetic information.

Molecular biologists now believed they had the basic framework of genetics in place; only the details needed to be added. Their work was focused on the simplest and smallest living things that they could find—bacteria. In addition, they studied bacteriophages, viruses that infect and grow in bacteria. But, as it turned out, the answers were not as simple as they seemed. Genes could do some things the molecular biologists did not yet acknowledge, and Barbara's continuing work eventually would fit into the complicated hereditary picture.

She realized DNA was important. But she also believed that in concentrating so narrowly on this part of genetics, geneticists were forgetting the larger picture. After all, DNA research had not succeeded in explaining processes such as the "turning on" and "turning off" of genes that she was observing in maize chromosomes. In fact, in her research during the 1950s, she found entirely new systems of genetic regulation and control in addition to the AC and DS system she had discovered earlier.

Between 1958 and 1960, a different job challenged her. At the invitation of the National Academy of Sciences, she spent two winters in Central and South America training Latin American scientists to collect and identify maize plants native to this region of the world.

Recognizing a Genetic Giant

During the next decade, the 1960s, new evidence showed that certain elements in bacteria were similar to the controlling elements Barbara had found in maize. And, in the early 1970s, experiments with the DNA of a common bacteria, *Escherichia coli* (better known as *E. coli*), revealed the same kinds of genetic rearrangement Barbara had identified in maize. It took a while longer, but geneticists finally agreed that transposition occurs in complex organisms, including humans.

Widespread acknowledgment of Barbara's earlier work on transposition came in the mid 1970s. The maize plant, ignored by so many researchers for so long, attracted attention. What was more, geneticists found that those who work on the molecular level and those, like Barbara, who stress the importance of the complete life form are studying two aspects of the same scientific puzzle.

Since 1980 the field of genetics has gone though a knowledge explosion. Advance has followed advance so quickly that no one can predict what will happen next. Scientists are "engineering," or bringing about, genetic changes that would have been thought impossible only a short time ago.

Meanwhile, Barbara continues to study the exchange of genetic material as it occurs in nature. She is particularly fascinated by the possibility of transferring genetic material from one species to another. One of her recent studies involves a kind of wasp that deposits its eggs in plant tissues. This part of the plant then forms a protective growth, called a gall, around the eggs. Barbara suspects that the stimulus provided by the wasp forces a change in the plant's genetic structure, causing the formation of the galls.

During the first years of the 1980s, Barbara received an extraordinary number of awards. All at once everyone seemed to realize the importance of her work and wanted to express their appreciation. In just two years, 1981 and 1982, she received eight major awards. For instance, the John D. and Catherine T. MacArthur Foundation chose her to be its first prize Fellow Laureate, guaranteeing her an income of $60,000 a year tax free for life. She also received the $15,000 Albert Lasker Basic Medical Research Award, and a $50,000 prize from Israel's Wolf Foundation.

In a press conference she gave at the time she learned of the MacArthur Foundation's decision, she said, "It's too much at once. I'm seventy-nine and at my age I should be allowed to do as I please and have my fun."

In spite of her dedication to her work, Barbara has kept her sense of humor. If something amuses her she "gets the giggles" like a child. In fact, she recently told a friend that her dreams are so funny that she sometimes laughs out loud in the night, waking herself from sleep. Playing a joke appeals to her, for she likes doing the unexpected.

One day, for instance, a photographer came to take pictures of her in her laboratory. When she is not using her microscopes, they are covered with bags to protect them from dust. As soon as the photographer was ready, Barbara quickly grabbed a bag from on top of one of the microscopes and stuck it over her head. Unable to stop in time, the photographer took the picture anyway.

A Prize for the Maize Scientist

While many Nobel winners learn of their honor when a reporter calls them, Barbara has no phone. She found out when she listened to a radio broadcast in October 1983. Her response was characteristic: she went out to pick walnuts on a path near her apartment in Cold Spring Harbor. Unlike some other laureates who rushed home to change clothes, Barbara kept on her usual casual but neat outfit—jeans, a shirt and sweater, and comfortable walking shoes.

A great many Nobel winners praise their coworkers, but Barbara—although helped by friends and faithfully supported by the Carnegie Institution of Washington—had done her Nobel work alone. When she met with the press, she chose to praise her corn. She said, "The prize is such an extraordinary honor. It might seem unfair, however, to reward a person for having so much pleasure over the years, asking the maize plant to solve specific problems and then watching its responses."

Barbara's Nobel award was unusual for many reasons. For one thing, it honored work she had begun four decades earlier. In addition, she became the first woman ever to win an unshared Nobel Prize in physiology or medicine. Only two other women, Marie Curie in 1911 and Dorothy Hodgkin in 1964, had won unshared prizes in any of the science categories recognized by Nobel Prizes.

Barbara invited three people to come with her to Stockholm, Sweden, when she traveled there to accept the Nobel Prize: her niece, Marjorie Bhavnani, Marjorie's husband Ashok, and their son, Raoul. The Concert Hall, where the prizes are given, was filled with row upon row of invited guests, all dressed in fancy evening wear. After the king and queen of Sweden had taken their seats, trumpets announced the entrance of the Nobel winners. The ceremony opened with short descriptions of each laureate's achievements. Then the awards began. Between each award, music relating to Alfred Nobel's life was played, a reminder that 1983 marked the 150th anniversary of his birth.

When Barbara accepted her award, the applause grew louder and louder until the floor of the Concert Hall vibrated. Usually the audience at a Nobel ceremony is fairly formal and reserved. This time, though, the people's imagination had been captured by the life and work of the small elderly woman standing on the stage.

Later, at the dinner and dance at the Town Hall, Barbara left her seat of honor next to the king. It was time for the three-minute speech winners give on this occasion. According to a Carnegie trustee who was there, she spoke of the joys of working alone. She also gave a Nobel lecture later the same week, but—with a touch of the stubbornness that she shows from time to time—at first she refused requests to make public the contents of her lecture.

Looking to the Future

Today Barbara continues to work with maize. She has gathered enough data to keep her going into the next century. In the year 2000 she would be ninety-eight, but those who know her think she probably will be right there celebrating on that memorable New Year's Eve.

Barbara goes on learning more about genes and their ability to control life processes. Many applications of her work have been made, and more are expected. Recent evidence shows that moveable genetic elements may be involved in changing normal cells into those that form cancers. Another aspect of her research reveals that controlling elements tend to change position more quickly following stress on a life form. Depending on the life form, stress could include any number of events, such as a reduced amount of food or sudden temperature changes. Barbara believes that response to stress may account for sudden (in biological terms this can mean thousands of years) changes in species or the development of new ones.

Throughout her career she has enjoyed learning about the work of young researchers. Whenever she visits a university, she spends more time with the students than with their teachers. And, at Cold Spring Harbor, she always has had a few young geneticists working with her.

When Barbara looks to the future, she hopes the next generation of scientists will remember not to narrow their vision. Instead, she thinks they should be familiar with more than one scientific field. Then, if they keep their minds open, they will be able to find connections they may otherwise miss. This is what she herself succeeded in doing.

She especially hopes scientists will have a love of nature—that they will observe and record what goes on in the natural areas around them. Modern science had its beginnings in such work, and Barbara believes that the tradition should be carried on. If it is not, she fears we will forget that what happens in laboratories is only a reflection of a larger, more complex world.

However, each scientific investigator must find his or her own way of working. Barbara found hers and had the confidence to stay with it. Certainly, her unique style of thinking and expression sometimes got in the way of her ability to win acceptance for her work. But she wanted to do her research more than anything else, and she knew that what she was finding out was important. In the long run, that was all that mattered.

Appendix A
Other
Nobel-Winning
Women

Eight women Nobel winners are included in this book. Their lives are of particular interest to teenage readers. The other Nobel women, however, also have done interesting work and led exciting lives. Here are short descriptions of them. Keep in mind that each year one or more women's names may be added.

Mairead Corrigan (1944-   ) and
Betty Williams (1943-   ) Irish
Peace Prize 1976 (award delayed until 1977)

On August 10, 1976, in Belfast, Northern Ireland, a car driven by a member of the Irish Republican Army went out of control when its driver was shot by British soldiers. The car crossed a sidewalk and killed three children and seriously injured their mother, Anne Maguire. Although Anne survived her injuries, she later committed suicide in grief over

223

the deaths of her children. These deaths were only the most recent in Ireland's long civil war—a bitter struggle involving religious and political beliefs rooted in the country's past.

Out of this tragedy, however, came a bond of friendship and a determination to stop the killings. Anne's sister, Mairead Corrigan, went on television to plead for an end to violence. Soon she heard that another woman, Betty Williams, was organizing a peace rally. When the two women met, they joined forces and organized an impressive peace movement with marches and meetings that received newspaper headlines around the world. Money and support poured into the headquarters of the "Community of the Peace People" as the movement came to be known. Some who had been bitter enemies began to talk with one another, and many hoped an end to bloodshed might be in sight.

Their work won them the Nobel Prize. But, for a variety of reasons, the movement Mairead Corrigan and Betty Williams founded lost much of its appeal. The prize also had an effect on both women's personal lives. There are still many people working for peace in Northern Ireland, however, and the efforts and hopes of the Peace People have not been forgotten.

Gerty Cori (1896-1957)   American
Physiology or Medicine Prize 1947 together with her husband Carl Cori and shared with Bernardo Houssay

Both Gerty and Carl were born in Czechoslovakia and came to the United States in 1922. Later they became naturalized citizens. They won the Nobel Prize for their contributions to biochemistry, especially for research on carbohydrate metabolism and enzymes. The Coris worked both as a team and on individual research. Gerty was professor of biological chemistry at Washington University, Saint Louis, Missouri, where Carl also held a professorship.

Gerty showed great courage when she continued to work in the laboratory for ten years with a crippling bone-marrow disease. The Coris were praised at the Nobel ceremony for their "unusual intuition and technical skill."

Emily Balch (1867-1961)   American
Peace Prize 1946 shared with John Mott

Emily grew up in a close-knit New England family. She became an outstanding member of Bryn Mawr College's first graduating class and was awarded a year of study in Paris. Back in America, she met Jane Addams, who was to win the 1931 Nobel Peace Prize.

Emily decided on a career as a college teacher and eventually became head of the department of economics and sociology at Wellesley College. She also worked to give women the right to vote and spoke out against racial prejudice. In 1903 she helped found the Women's Labor Union League, which organized women wage earners into trade unions so that they could have a better chance for fair pay and improved working conditions.

With the outbreak of World War I, Emily began another career—that of peace worker. She traveled to Europe with other women seeking peace and talked with high-ranking officials. Her work once again brought her in contact with Jane Addams, and the two became long-term coworkers and friends.

In 1919 she became secretary/treasurer of the Women's International League for Peace and Freedom. Throughout the 1920s and 30s, she continued to work for peace. She also tried to find time to write, for she kept diaries and journals and was the author of well-received books.

When Emily learned she was the winner of the Nobel Peace Prize, she was ill in a hospital. But, a year later, she went to Norway to give her Nobel lecture and was honored in London with a gala dinner. Even in her eighties she traveled, wrote, and promoted peace efforts. She died one day after her ninety-fourth birthday.

Gabriela Mistral (1889-1957)   Chilean Literature Prize 1945

Gabriela Mistral was the pen name assumed by a young Chilean schoolteacher. She taught in rural schools before receiving more prominent positions as an educator. Gabriela achieved recognition for her revision of the Mexican school system. In Latin America and European cities she served as an official of the Chilean government and represented her country at the League of Nations and the United Nations. She also lived in the United States for a time.

Her early poetry, full of the tragedy and sadness that touched her life many times, soon won her awards. When he was sixteen, Pablo Neruda, another Chilean poet who would later win the Nobel Literature Prize, became her friend. Her later poems revealed the tenderness of a mother's love as well as a strong desire for social justice.

Sonetos de la Muerte ("Sonnets of Death") is considered one of her finest poetry collections. *Desolación*, *Tala*, and

Lagar are three of her major volumes. *Selected Poems*, translated by the American black poet Langston Hughes, appeared the year Gabriela died.

Irène Joliot-Curie (1897-1956)   French
Chemistry Prize 1935 together with her husband, Frédéric Joliot-Curie

Twenty-four years after Irène watched her mother, Marie, accept her Nobel Chemistry Prize, she returned to Stockholm to share this same award with her husband, Frédéric. Marie and Irène remain the only mother and daughter to have won Nobel prizes.

Irène and Frédéric shared a love of mountain climbing and swimming while they continued the work Irène's parents had begun on radioactivity. They worked at the Radium Institute in Paris where Irène succeeded her mother as director in 1932. Their research led them to the production of the first artificial radioactive substances. In 1940 they worked together in research on the chain reaction in nuclear fission. Irène took a keen interest in the social and intellectual advancement of women.

Jane Addams (1860-1935)   American
Peace Prize 1931 shared with Nicholas Murray Butler

A leader in the fight to win voting rights for women and a vigorous worker in the peace movement, Jane Addams is best known for the founding of Hull House in Chicago.

At this community center the working-class people of the

neighborhood—many of them immigrants—could learn skills, find help for their problems, and relax with friends. Young women made Hull House their residence, enabling them to hold jobs for the first time. Later, Hull House also served as a center for social reform activities. Many similar settlement houses were established.

By the time of her death, Jane Addams had touched the lives of millions of people. Possibly her greatest contribution was making social work a profession. Professional social workers are now trained in universities to understand the economic, social, and psychological causes of city problems. Jane Addams' books include *The Spirit of Youth and the City Streets*, *A New Conscience and an Ancient Evil*, and *Twenty Years at Hull-House*.

Sigrid Undset (1882-1949)   Norwegian Literature Prize 1928

The Nobel Prize was given to Sigrid Undset for her "powerful descriptions" of life during the Middle Ages. Her early novels, however, used a modern setting. *Jenny*, which appeared in 1911, described a love affair in terms that were, for their time, very direct. This book created a sensation and was her first success.

After her conversion to Roman Catholicism, her writing, which had always been concerned with morals, became more intensely religious. *Kristin Lavransdatter*, considered her masterpiece, told of love and religion in medieval Norway. Her later works returned to stories of modern life. *The Faithful Wife* and the autobiographical *The Longest Years* were written during this period. Sigrid came to the United States after the

Nazi invasion of Norway and returned home in 1945.

Grazia Deledda (1875-1936)   Italian
Literature Prize 1926

A novelist, Grazia Deledda's first work, a collection of short stories, was published when she was nineteen. Her early life was filled with family tragedies. Lyric and naturalistic, her novels combine a deep understanding of human nature with touches of humor and violence. *Dopo il Divorzio* ("After the Divorce"), *Canne al Vento* ("Reeds in the Wind"), and *La Madre* ("The Mother") are some of her better-known works.

Selma Lagerlöf (1858-1940)   Swedish
Literature Prize 1909

Selma Lagerlöf was in her early twenties, working as a teacher, when she decided to write about the legends and folklore of Värmland, the region in Sweden where she had grown up. She had heard such tales many times from her father and grandmother. The novel she began, *The Story of Gösta Berling*, told of the adventures of a priest who had lost the right to practice his religion. When the first three chapters won a magazine competition, she decided to finish the book. Later she remembered the time when she wrote this novel as the happiest of her life. She went on to write other books, including *Jerusalem* and *The Ring of the Lowenskolds*. Lagerlöf's short stories, *The Wonderful Adventures of Nils*, are considered children's classics.

Lame since she was three, she nevertheless was an imposing figure when she crossed the stage in Stockholm to become the first woman to win the Nobel Literature Prize. The year before her death she helped Nelly Sachs escape from Nazi Germany. A little more than a quarter of a century later, Nelly also won the Literature Prize.

Bertha von Suttner (1843-1914)   Austrian
Peace Prize 1905

Born an aristocrat in Prague, Bertha became a governess to the von Suttner family in Vienna when her family's fortunes took a downturn. While working there, at the age of thirty, she fell in love with one of the von Suttner sons, Artur, who was seven years younger. When Artur told his parents he wanted to marry Bertha, the von Suttners objected. Wanting to get rid of the governess, they helped her look for a new position as a secretary in Paris. When Bertha arrived to discuss the job, she discovered her possible employer was Alfred Nobel, the well-known inventor. Nobel was attracted to her, but after only a week he left for the opening of one of his factories. While he was gone, Bertha and Artur managed to see each other and were secretly married. It is thought that Nobel, who never married, might have proposed to Bertha if he had had the chance.

Disowned by Artur's family, Bertha and her husband had to earn their living in Russia by teaching and writing. In 1889 Bertha's book, *Lay Down Your Arms*, a powerful attack on the horrors of war, was a worldwide success. It told the story of Martha, a young soldier's wife, who learns from firsthand experience that the so-called "glories" of war can bring terrible suffering. Bertha also edited a peace journal, attended peace conferences, and gave lectures. She spoke out against the Boer and Spanish-American Wars. One week before World War I began, she died.

Bertha's friendship with Nobel continued, mostly through letters, after her marriage. Many people believed that he established the Peace Prize partly because of her influence. In 1905 she became the first woman to win this award.

Marie Curie (1867-1934)   French
Physics Prize 1903 together with her husband Pierre Curie and shared with Antoine Becquerel
Chemistry Prize 1911

Marie's interest in science was encouraged by her father, a professor of physics in Warsaw. In 1891 Marie went to Paris to attend the famous school known as the Sorbonne. She married Pierre Curie four years later and began her research independently in his laboratory. Following Becquerel's discovery of radioactivity, Marie and Pierre joined their research. They discovered polonium and radium and, by refusing to patent their processes, passed up any commercial gain from their work. The Curies shared the Nobel Prize in physics in 1903. After Pierre's death in a street accident, Marie assumed his position at the Sorbonne.

In 1911 Marie received her second Nobel Prize, this time in chemistry. She was, at that time, the only person to have won two Nobel awards. She remains the only woman to have won twice. Watching from the audience when Marie accepted her second prize was her fourteen-year-old daughter, Irène. (See Irene Joliet-Curie above).

Appendix B
Complete List of Women Nobel Winners
(By Award Date)

1903	Physics	**Marie Curie** (1867-1934) and Pierre Curie (1859-1906)—French Shared with Antoine H. Becquerel—French
1905	Peace	**Bertha von Suttner** (1843-1914)—Austrian
1909	Literature	**Selma Lagerlöf** (1858-1940)—Swedish
1911	Chemistry	**Marie Curie** (1867-1934)—French
1926	Literature	**Grazia Deledda** (1875-1936)—Italian
1928	Literature	**Sigrid Undset** (1882-1949)—Norwegian
1931	Peace	**Jane Addams** (1860-1935)—American Shared with Nicholas Murray Butler—American

232

1935	_Chemistry_	**Irène Joliot-Curie** (1897-1956) and Frédéric Joliot-Curie (1900-1958)— French
1938	_Literature_	**Pearl S. Buck** (1892-1973)—American
1945	_Literature_	**Gabriela Mistral** (1889-1957)—Chilean
1946	_Peace_	**Emily Balch** (1867-1961)—American Shared with John Mott—American
1947	_Physiology or Medicine_	**Gerty T. Cori** (1896-1957) and Carl F. Cori (1896-1984)—American (b. Czechoslovakia) Shared with Bernardo Houssay—Argentinean
1963	_Physics_	**Maria Goeppert Mayer** (1906-1972)—American (b. Poland) Shared with Eugene P. Wigner—American (b. Hungary) and J. Hans D. Jensen—German
1964	_Chemistry_	**Dorothy C. Hodgkin** (1910-)— British
1966	_Literature_	**Nelly Sachs** (1891-1970)—Swedish (b. Germany) Shared with Shmuel Y. Agnon—Israeli
1976	_Peace_	**Betty Williams** (1943-) and **Mairead Corrigan** (1944-)—Irish Award delayed until 1977
1977	_Physiology or Medicine_	**Rosalyn Sussman Yalow** (1921-)—American Shared with Andrew Vincent Schally—American and Roger Guillemin—American (b. France)

1979	*Peace*	**Mother Teresa** (Agnes Gonxha Bojaxhiu) (1910-)—Indian (b. Albania now Yugoslavia)
1982	*Peace*	**Alva Myrdal** (1902-)—Swedish Shared with Alfonso Garcia Robles—Mexican
1983	*Physiology or Medicine*	**Barbara McClintock** (1902-)—American

Suggested Reading

Nelly Sachs

Current Biography Yearbook. New York: H. W. Wilson, 1967, p. 365. Three-page description of Sachs' life and work. At the end of this account, look for additional references about various aspects of her poetry and events in her life in Germany and Sweden.

Fox, Sylvan. "Nelly Sachs, Poet, Dead at 78; Won Nobel Prize for Literature." *The New York Times*, May 13, 1970, p. 41. Sachs' obituary.

Lagercrantz, Olof. "The Language of Suffering." *The Washington Post* (Book Week), July 9, 1967, p. 6. Especially good discussion of Sachs' poetry, including themes and images.

Sachs, Nelly. *O The Chimneys*, 1967, and *The Seeker*, 1970. New York: Farrar, Straus and Giroux. These two books contain Sachs' poems. In addition, *O The Chimneys* includes *Eli*, a verse play.

Rosalyn S. Yalow

Current Biography Yearbook. New York: H. W. Wilson, 1978, p. 458. Three-page description of Yalow's life and work. Look at additional references given at the end of this account.

Haber, Louis. *Women Pioneers of Science*. New York: Harcourt Brace Jovanovich, 1979. This book is written for young people. Be sure to look at the bibliography and lists at the back.

Les Prix Nobel en 1977. Stockholm, Sweden: Almqvist & Wiksell International. Official record of the Nobel Prizes; appears annually. This volume contains a good autobiography by Yalow.

Stone, Elizabeth. "A Mme. Curie From the Bronx." *The New York Times*, April 9, 1978, p. 37. Informative article on Yalow's career.

Alva Myrdal

Bird, David. "Stubborn Combatants in Disarmament's Cause." *The New York Times*, October 14, 1982, p. 10. Summary of Myrdal's life and work.

Myrdal, Alva. *The Game of Disarmament*. New York: Pantheon Books, 1982. Myrdal's account of the two superpowers' ability to block the efforts of people and nations seeking disarmament.

————. *Nation and Family*. Cambridge, Mass.: The M.I.T. Press, 1968. Explanation of Sweden's family and population policies. Foreword by Daniel P. Moynihan.

"Two Disarming Choices." *Time*, October 25, 1982, p. 52. Description of Myrdal's career that describes in particular her contribution to worldwide peacemaking.

Maria Goeppert Mayer

Dash, Joan. *A Life of One's Own.* New York: Harper & Row, 1973. This book includes biographies of three women: Margaret Sanger, Edna St. Vincent Millay, and Maria Goeppert Mayer. It is the single best source for information on Maria Goeppert Mayer and includes a good bibliography. The writing style is clear and interesting.

Fermi, Laura. *Atoms in the Family.* Chicago: The University of Chicago Press, 1954. Written by the wife of Enrico Fermi, the Nobel-winning physicist, this book appeared on the best-seller list the week Enrico died of cancer. It is a well written and amusing account of the Fermis' life and includes comments on Maria Goeppert Mayer and her husband. The author captures the excitement felt by those whose work ushered in the atomic era.

Hall, Mary Harrington. "An American Mother and the Nobel Prize." *McCall's*, July 1964, p. 38. Account of Maria Goeppert Mayer's life and work.

"Just Ask Mrs. Mayer." *Newsweek*, November 18, 1963, p. 78. Short description of Maria Goeppert Mayer's feelings when she heard she had won the Nobel Prize. Also includes a brief account of her work.

Pearl S. Buck

Block, Irvin. *The Lives of Pearl Buck.* New York: Thomas Y. Crowell Company, 1973. This is a biography written for young readers. The book's final chapter contains an interview the author had with Buck before her death.

Buck, Pearl S. *The Exile.* New York: The John Day Company in association with Reynal & Hitchcock, 1936. Buck's biography of her mother.

———. *Fighting Angel.* New York: The John Day Company in association with Reynal & Hitchcock, 1936. Buck's biography of her father.

———. *The Good Earth.* New York: The John Day Company, 1931. Buck's most famous novel.

Stirling, Nora. *Pearl Buck: A Woman in Conflict.* Piscataway, N.J.: New Century Publishers, Inc., 1983. This biography, written for adults, gives the events of Buck's life in clear-cut fashion. The author relates Buck's relationships with the men who influenced her life and work. There also is an interesting account of Buck's later years. Read the bibliography at the back of this book.

Dorothy Crowfoot Hodgkin

"British Winner Is a Grandmother." *The New York Times,* October 30, 1964, p. 24. Summary of Hodgkin's life.

"The Chemistry-Minded Mother." *Time,* November 6, 1964, p. 41. Description of Hodgkin's personality and her laboratory at Oxford.

Opfell, Olga S. *The Lady Laureates: Women Who Have Won the Nobel Prize.* Metuchen, N.J.: The Scarecrow Press, 1978. This book includes seventeen women winners of the Nobel Prize and describes Hodgkin's life and work.

Les Prix Nobel en 1964. Stockholm, Sweden: P. A. Norstedt & Söner, 1965. Official record of the Nobel Prizes; appears annually. This volume includes speeches made when Hodgkin received the Nobel Prize.

Mother Teresa

Kaufman, Michael T. "The World of Mother Teresa." *The New York Times Magazine*, December 9, 1979, p. 42. Description of Mother Teresa's life and work with interesting short stories about individuals she has worked with and those she has helped.

Pepper, Curtis Bill. "I'm a Little Pencil in God's Hand." *McCall's*, March 1980, p. 73. Based on an interview with Mother Teresa, this article gives insights into her life.

Serrou, Robert. *Teresa of Calcutta*. Maidenhead, England: McGraw-Hill Book Company (UK) Limited, 1980.* Informative chapters on Mother Teresa's life, including remarks by her brother. Detailed descriptions of all aspects of her work as well as a list of awards she has received.

Mother Teresa. *The Love of Christ*. New York: Harper & Row, 1982. Mother Teresa's own words as gathered from her speeches, letters, and other sources.

Barbara McClintock

Altman, Lawrence K. "Long Island Woman Wins Nobel in Medicine." *The New York Times*, October 11, 1983, p. 1. Description of McClintock's work with an easy-to-understand diagram.

Clark, Matt, and Shapiro, Dan. "The Kernel of Genetics." *Newsweek*, November 30, 1981, p. 74. Explanation of McClintock's investigation of shifting genes.

Keller, Evelyn Fox. *A Feeling for the Organism*. New York: W. H. Freeman, 1983. Comprehensive biography of McClintock.

*Quotations in the text marked by asterisks are from *Teresa of Calcutta*, by Robert Serrou.

Lewin, Roger. "A Naturalist of the Genome." *Science* 222 (28 October 1983):402-405. Account of McClintock's career and discussion of her experiments.

Miller, J. A. "Nobel Prize to McClintock and Her Mobile Elements." *Science News* 124 (15 October 1983):244. Diagrams of shifting genes and the maize plant as well as brief article on McClintock's work.

Bibliography

The lives of Nobel winners are fascinating to research. Readers who are interested in finding out more about one or more laureates can use this bibliography in addition to the suggested reading list.

Writings by the Nobel winners in addition to those given below may be found by using local library cards and/or microform catalogs, *Books in Print* (New York: R. R. Bowker), and *Readers' Guide to Periodical Literature* (New York: H. W. Wilson) as well as more specialized periodical indexes.

The following list provides a beginning for locating materials about the women Nobel winners. Many more sources are available. Your reference librarian is the best person to ask for help. Each field in which Nobel Prizes are awarded (physics, literature, etc.) has special texts and guides. In addition, investigation of subject headings such as "women in the sciences" can provide research opportunities. Indexes to major newspapers also are valuable as are such quick reference sources as encyclopedias and almanacs.

General Texts and Sources

Current Biography. New York: H. W. Wilson. Appears monthly and is then bound into an annual Yearbook.

Ireland, Norma Olin. *Index to Women of the World from Ancient to Modern Times: Biographies and Portraits.* Westwood, Mass.: F. W. Faxon, 1970.

Nobelstiftelsen, Stockholm. *Les Prix Nobel*: Nobel Prizes, presentations, biographies, and lectures. Stockholm: Almqvist & Wiksell International, 1904-present (coverage from 1901). The official record of the Nobel Prizes. Contains an account of the ceremonies, each recipient's Nobel lecture, and a biography of each winner. The lectures are generally in the original language, though in recent years translations usually have been provided.

Notable American Women: The Modern Period: A Biographical Dictionary. Edited by Barbara Sicherman and Carol Hurd Green. Cambridge, Mass.: Belknap Press of Harvard University Press, 1980.

Opfell, Olga S. *The Lady Laureates: Women Who Have Won the Nobel Prize.* Metuchen, N.J.: Scarecrow Press, 1978.

Women's History Sources: A Guide to Archives and Manuscript Collections in the United States. Edited by Andrea Hinding in association with the University of Minnesota. New York: R. R. Bowker, 1979.

Zuckerman, Harriet. *Scientific Elite: Nobel Laureates in the United States.* New York: Free Press, 1977.

Alfred Nobel and the Nobel Prizes

Sources for Alfred Nobel and the establishment of his prizes are given below, followed by additional references for each woman winner in this book.

Meyer, Edith Patterson. *In Search of Peace.* Nashville:

Abingdon, 1978.

Nobelstiftelsen, Stockholm. *Nobel, The Man and His Prizes.* 3rd ed. New York: American Elsevier, 1972.

Riedman, Sarah, and Gustafson, Elton. *Portraits of Nobel Laureates in Medicine and Physiology.* New York: Abelard-Schuman, 1963.

Swedish Consulate General, Information Service, 825 Third Avenue, New York City.

Swedish Embassy, library, 600 New Hampshire Avenue, NW, Washington, D.C.

Tolf, Robert W. *The Russian Rockefellers.* Stanford, California: Hoover Institution Press, Stanford University, 1976.

Nelly Sachs

The Leo Baeck Institute, Archives, 129 East 73rd Street, New York City.

Bosmajian, Hamida. *Metaphors of Evil: Contemporary German Literature and the Shadow of Nazism.* Iowa City: University of Iowa Press, 1979.

Dodds, Dinah. "The Process of Renewal in Nelly Sachs' Eli." *The German Quarterly* 49 (January 1976):50-58.

Friedlander, Albert Hoschander. "Nelly Sachs: Poet of the Holocaust." *The Jewish Quarterly* 14 (Winter 1966-67):6-8.

Langer, Lawrence. "Nelly Sachs." *Colloquia Germanica* 10 (1976-77):316-325.

Sachs, Nelly. *O The Chimneys.* New York: Farrar, Straus and Giroux, 1967.

_____. *The Seeker.* New York: Farrar, Straus and Giroux, 1970.

Schwebell, Gertrude C. "Nelly Sachs." *Saturday Review* 49 (10 December 1966):46-47.

Rosalyn S. Yalow

Bauman, William A., and Yalow, Rosalyn S. "Child Abuse: Parenteral Insulin Administration." *The Journal of Pediatrics* 99 (October 1981):588-591.

Kent, Leticia. "Winner Woman." *Vogue*, January 1978, p. 131.

Stone, Elizabeth. "A Mme. Curie from the Bronx." *The New York Times Magazine*, April 9, 1978, p. 37.

Warsaw, Jacqueline. " ' To Commit Is To Achieve' says Rosalyn Yalow, Winner of the Nobel Prize in Medicine (1977)." *Working Woman*, May 1978, p. 47.

Yalow, Rosalyn S. "Radioactivity in the Service of Man." *Bioscience* 31 (January 1981):23-28.

_____. "Radioimmunoassay: A Probe for the Fine Structure of Biologic Systems." *Science* 200 (16 June 1978): 1236-1245.

Yalow, Rosalyn S., and Eng, J. "Peptide Hormones in Strange Places—Are They There?" *Peptides* 2 (1981):17-23.

Alva Myrdal

Arbetarrörelsens Arkiv, Stockholm, Sweden (Upplandsgatan 5, Box 1124, 111 81 Stockholm). This archives is the primary repository for materials concerning Alva and Gunnar Myrdal.

Carlson, Allan C. "The Roles of Alva and Gunnar Myrdal in the Development of a Social Democratic Response to Europe's 'Population Crisis,' 1929-1938." Ph.D. dissertation, Ohio University, 1978. Library of Congress Microform AAD 78-21174.

Contemporary Authors, vol. 69-72. Detroit: Gale Research, 1978, p. 448.

Kellgren, Nils. "Brutaliteten och våldet från de rika länderna är det hemska i vår tid." ["The Most Horrible Aspect of Our Time is the Brutality and Violence of the Affluent Countries."] *Fackföreningsrörelsen* 1973:13A, p. 16.

Lindskog, Lars. *Alva Myrdal.* Stockholm: Sveriges Radios, 1981.

Link, Ruth. "Alva." *Sweden Now* 1976:3, p. 39.

Myrdal, Alva. *The Game of Disarmament.* New York: Pantheon Books, 1976.

Maria Goeppert Mayer

Born, Max. *My Life.* New York: Scribner's, 1975.

Columbia Oral History Collection, Columbia University, New York City.

Dash, Joan. *A Life of One's Own.* New York: Harper & Row, 1973.

Fermi, Laura. *Atoms in the Family.* Chicago: The University of Chicago Press, 1954.

Mayer, Maria G. "The Structure of the Nucleus." *Scientific American* 184 (March 1951):22-26.

Sachs, Robert G. "Maria Goeppert Mayer." In *Biographical Memoirs,* vol. 50, Washington, D.C.: National Academy of Sciences, 1979, pp. 311-328.

Pearl S. Buck

Buck, Pearl S. *The Exile.* New York: The John Day Company in association with Reynal & Hitchcock, 1936.

_____. *Fighting Angel.* New York: The John Day Company in association with Reynal & Hitchcock, 1936.

_____. *The Good Earth.* New York: The John Day Company, 1931.

French, Warren G., and Kidd, Walter E., eds. *American Winners of the Nobel Literary Prize.* Norman: University of Oklahoma Press, 1968.

Harris, Theodore F. *Pearl Buck.* New York: John Day, vol. 1, 1969, vol. 2, 1971.

Snow, Helen F. "Pearl S. Buck 1892-1973." *The New Republic,* March 24, 1973, pp. 28-29.

Spencer, Cornelia [Grace Sydenstricker Yaukey]. *The Exile's Daughter.* New York: Coward-McCann, 1944.

Stirling, Nora. *Pearl Buck: A Woman in Conflict.* Piscataway, N.J.: New Century Publishers, 1983.

Woolf, S. J. "Pearl Buck Finds that East and West Do Meet." *The New York Times Magazine,* November 20, 1938, p. 4.

Dorothy Crowfoot Hodgkin

Dodson, Guy; Glusker, Jenny; and Sayre, David, eds. *Structural Studies on Molecules of Biological Interest* (a volume in honor of Dorothy Hodgkin). New York: Oxford University Press, 1981.

Fishlock, David. "Insulin Design Traced." *Science News* 96 (4 October 1969):307.

Hodgkin, Dorothy C. "Crystallographic Measurements and the Structure of Protein Molecules as They Are." *Annals of the New York Academy of Sciences* 325 (May 1979): 121-148.

Jeffery, G. A. "Nobel Prize in Chemistry Awarded to Crystallographer." *Science* 146 (6 November 1964):748-749.

Judson, Horace Freeland. *The Eighth Day of Creation.* New York: Simon and Schuster, 1979.

Mother Teresa

Le Joly, E. *We Do It for Jesus.* London: Darton, Longman and Todd, Ltd., 1977.

Muggeridge, Malcolm. *Something Beautiful for God.* New

246

York: Harper & Row, 1971.

Serrou, Robert. *Teresa of Calcutta.* New York: McGraw-Hill, 1980.

Spink, Kathryn. *The Miracle of Love.* New York: Harper & Row, 1981.

Teresa, Mother. *A Gift for God.* New York: Harper & Row, 1980.

Barbara McClintock

Cold Spring Harbor Laboratory, Archives, Cold Spring Harbor, New York.

Keller, Evelyn Fox. *A Feeling for the Organism.* New York: W. H. Freeman, 1983.

McClintock, Barbara. "Induction of Instability of Selected Loci in Maize." *Genetics* 38 (1953):579-599.

Maranto, Gina. "At Long Last—A Nobel for a Loner." *Discover,* December 1983, p. 26.

Talan, Jamie. "Organisms Speak for Nobel Winner." *The New York Times,* Long Island Weekly Section, October 16, 1983, p. 23.

Veronda, Winifred. "James Bonner Recalls Nobel Laureate Barbara McClintock." *Cal Tech News* 18 (February 1984):3 (California Institute of Technology).

Index

play, 137
Gromyko, Andrei, 83
Guillemin, Dr. Roger, 58
Gustaf, King, 42-43

Herzfeld, Karl, 99
Hocking, Ernest, 145
Hodgkin, Dorothy Crowfoot:
at Cambridge, 153; child-
hood of, 148-149; children
of, 155, 162; honors and
awards, 159, 163; insulin
and, 163; marriage of, 155;
Nobel Prize and, 162-163;
at Oxford, 151, 153, 156,
158, 162; penicillin and,
156-158; vitamin B-12 and,
159-161
Hodgkin, Thomas, 155, 161-
162
Home for the Dying, 179
House Divided, A, 136
Houssay, Bernardo, 224
Hull House, 227

Imperial Woman, 144
International Federation of
Business and Professional
Women, 78
Irish Republican Army, 223

Jenny, 227
Jensen, Hans, 110-111

Jerusalem, 229
John Paul II, Pope, 192
Joliot-Curie, Frédéric, 85,
226-227
Joliot-Curie, Irène, 85, 226-
227, 231
*Journal of Clinical Investiga-
tion,* 53

Kissinger, Henry, 83
Kristin Lavransdatter, 228

Lagar, 226
Lagerlöf, Selma, 29, 32, 35
36, 228-229
Lay Down Your Arms, 229
League of Nations, 72
Legends and Tales, 32
Longest Years, The, 228
Low, Barbara, 156-157

McClintock, Barbara: at Cal
Tech, 206-207; childhood
of, 198-199; at Cold Springs
Harbor, 209-212; at Cor-
nell, 201; gall formation
and, 217; honors and a-
wards, 207-208, 211, 215,
218; meiosis and, 205; Nobel Prize and, 218-220; response to stress and, 220-
221; at University of Missouri, 206-209

maize genetics: beginnings of, 202; chromosomes and, 202-203, 209; DNA and, 211, 216-217; mutation and, 213; *Neurospora* and, 212; pollination and, 205; *transposition* and, 214

Mayer, Joseph, 89, 95, 97, 100, 102, 111

Mayer, Maria Goeppert: childhood of, 90-91; children of, 99-100, 106, 111-112; death of, 112; at Göttingen, 93; at Institute for Nuclear Studies, 105; at Johns Hopkins, 98; Manhattan Project and, 102-104; marriage of, 96; Nobel Prize and, 89, 111; spin-orbit coupling and, 107-110; World War II and, 101-104

Mendel, Gregor, 202

Missionaries of Charity: beginnings of, 176; children and, 180-181; dying and, 179; lepers and, 183-184; world expansion of, 181-182, 188, 191-193

Missionary Brothers of Charity, 187

Mistral, Gabriela, 226

molecular biology, 211, 216

Morgan, Thomas Hunt, 203, 206, 208

Mother, The, 136

Mott, John, 225

Myrdal, Alva: as ambassador to India, 80-81; in America, 70-71, 76, 79; children of, 72, 76; disarmament and, 82-83, 86; honors and awards, 70, 84; marriage of, 69; as member of Swedish parliament, 81; Nobel Prize and, 85-86; Social Democratic Party and, 74, 78; United Nations and, 79-81; women's rights and, 71, 74-75; World War II and, 76, 78

Myrdal, Gunnar, 69, 72-74, 80, 84

My Several Worlds, 144

National Academy of Science, 211, 216

Nation and Family, 77

Neruda, Pablo, 226

New Conscience and an Ancient Evil, A, 227

Nobel, Alfred: birth of, 15-17; discovery of dynamite,

The Author

Barbara Shiels is an established freelance writer/editor who writes on a variety of topics, including science and the arts. She received a grant from the American Association of University Women Educational Foundation to assist in the writing of this book. Ms. Shiels did extensive research at the Library of Congress, personally interviewed some of the Nobel-Prize-winning women and their friends, relatives, and colleagues, and had the biographies reviewed by the subjects themselves or experts in their fields.

Of the book, she says: "By reading about these famous women, perhaps young people—particularly girls—will understand that, even if they never win a Nobel Prize, the challenge of finding enjoyable work and learning to do it well can be its own reward. What is more, since some of the women winners juggled families and careers while others battled personal problems such as ill health or political persecution, their stories reveal real-life complications readers may face as they mature."

The author has worked as a copy and staff editor for World Publishing Company and Appleton-Century-Crofts, as a faculty research assistant for Dr. Louis Harlan at the University of Maryland, and as the director of the office of public information of the Washington, D.C., YWCA. Ms. Shiels graduated with honors from Connecticut College. A member of the Washington Independent Writers and the American Association of University Women, she lives in Reston, Virginia, with her husband and child.